SKETCHES OF BUTTE

by

George Wesley Davis

ISBN 10: 1494919184
ISBN 13: 978-1494919184

ANACONDA HILL
"The Richest Hill"

Sketches of Butte

(From Vigilante Days to Prohibition)

by

GEORGE WESLEY DAVIS

author of

"Dancing Girls of Cairo,"
"On the Danube and the Rhine"

THE CORNHILL COMPANY
BOSTON

FOREWORD

In writing these sketches, I have avoided, as much as possible, the over-written mines, courts and politics.

I shall give a pen picture of a wonderful Western camp, the good and bad of an unusual people, the joys and horrors of the largest mining camp in the world, a city of many contrasts.

The Butte of the early days is passing, and like many of what were once the frontier towns and camps of our great Western country, the picturesqueness of its life is passing with it, so that, even today, it seems necessary to make a narrative of personal experience or observation, as most old-timers of the "diggings" are averse to talking of early days, except in a general way. Perhaps it is because of a fear of throwing light on shadows of former days, a time when life was reckless. One must have lived in those days to picture it as it was from the beginning of the placer diggings down to the present day. It is my wish to be fair with all classes and give conditions as they have existed from year to year. I trust that this fact alone will justify my taking the reader from places of joy to sections where tragedy stalks about the streets.

Many of the great mining camps today are ghost towns—Bannack, Cripple Creek, Tonapah and Goldfields are scarcely more than memories of their tempestuous past, and their history has largely died with them. Butte alone remains individual, distinct, apart, greater today than ever before, a city now, although throughout the world referred to as a camp, the most wonderful the world has ever known, half ashamed of its past, yet like unto no other of our important cities.

George Wesley Davis.

CONTENTS

ILLUSTRATIONS

SKETCHES OF BUTTE

Chapter One

VIGILANTE DAYS

In the early sixties Montana was infested with bandits of the lowest type. The first successful reform movement was planned and accomplished by the Vigilantes. That was before my day in the west; a time when Henry Plummer and his associates terrorized Montana and Idaho.

I can best tell the story of the Vigilantes as it was told to me by one who lived in the territories in those days. He was an old man I met in the office of a little hotel in Virginia City who gave me the story of his early life. I had just returned from a walk down Alder gulch to Nevada, a camp two miles below, where, in early days, wild and picturesque characters panned gold. It was a fascinating walk as the sun's soft glow melted into twilight; sparkling waterfalls sang in the evening's quiet, and nature seemed a fairy dream.

At twilight here the world is mystic,
And the purple canyon seems
Brooding over the empty cabins
Ghostly in the pale moon-beams.

Here they flocked when life was cruel,
Rough hard men of rugged mould,
Driven to earth's farthest places
In their quest for harder gold.

But tonight stars blink and quiver,
And trees whispering seem to say,
"When gold failed they quickly left us
Here in solitude to stay."

As shadows deepened deserted cabins seemed weird in the mystic twilight. Trees with their fresh spring green sparkled like myriads of jewels, as stars broke through from above.

Being a lover of nature more than of the artificial life of the city, I walked slowly through the still canyon, but life's current ran swiftly in my veins. Pines whispered to the rippling waters, and the whole atmosphere was delightfully fascinating. White peaks, where the sunlight lingers long, were darkening as I reached the hotel. I bathed my hands in a basin of cold water that stood in a corner of the office, and dried them on a roll-towel that hung close by. The place was used as office, bar, and sitting-room. A barber's chair stood in one corner. Wooden cuspidors, with sawdust in them, were here and there about the floor, but the loungers seemed rather to try at hitting the stove which stood in the center of the smoke-filled place.

The old man who told me the story of the first Vigilance Committee was quick-witted and well read for one practically self-made. He was vigorous, but his shoulders were bent and many lines showed in his pleasant face.

He was a Mormon who had drifted away from the cold, commercial life of the colony at Salt Lake.

"The first name given to this camp," he said, launching into the story, "was Varina City. The name was given in honor of the wife of the Confederate President, Jefferson Davis, but afterwards was changed to Virginia City.

"My mother was a New England woman," he continued, "and imparted to me the love and affection of her people. She was never a Mormon at heart."

He sat for a moment, his eyes resting on the floor. I asked him why she married into the Mormon church. His answer was: "Please do not ask me." His sad voice dismissed the subject.

"My father," he said, "was an Englishman; strong mentally, but slight of physique. My mother was his fifth and last wife. By the five wives he had twenty-five children. All who lived were both mentally and physically strong, and, I think, above the average. When I was a boy just passing into manhood, my father talked to me of the future. I listened—that was all. He said to me that day: 'My son, you will soon have reached the age when it will be wise for you to take unto yourself a wife. I am going to tell you how I chose my wives, and I wish you to follow my example.'

"He told me how the sire gave the mental characteristics to a child, while the mother imparted the physical. As he finished he said, 'So, son, in selecting a wife, look for physical charms as a farmer would select a desirable spot for a garden. Do not allow that emotion the Gentiles call love to enter your mind.'

"While listening to him my thoughts went out to a little schoolmate. Although only a boy I loved the little girl devotedly and revolted at my father's suggestion."

"Did you marry her?" I interrupted.

"Yes," he smiled. "We kept our secret from the world, guarding it as we would a great treasure. When I reached the age of eighteen, my father again talked to me and suggested I take my first wife. I was then a man grown and fully able to provide a home."

"I suppose you were not long in deciding, were you?" I said, in a joking way.

"No," he smiled again. "She soon became my wife.

"As the colony at Salt Lake grew to be a city," he continued, "the people spread out to nearby territories, my people coming to this state—then a territory. We left Zion one morning at sunrise. My father, his wives and younger children, my wife and myself, comprised the little band that headed for Bannack, our future home. We were two months making the journey, for we suffered much from small bands of renegade Indians and often spent days in hiding. At such times it was necessary to blindfold our horses and muzzle their mouths, the covering being removed only when they were fed and watered, for their whinny would tell the Indians of our whereabouts.

"When on the march and camped for the night I would take my place at the edge of the little camp and sit with gun in hand during the long, lonesome hours of the night, guarding the loved ones while they slept and taking my rest during the day as we journeyed on. My wife drove the horses while I slept on the bed of the dead-ax wagon."

"Did you not have mattresses?" I asked.

"No," he laughed, "of course not. At first we had ticks filled with dried wild grass, but at different times when we were in hiding the contents of those ticks had to go to feed the horses, for they could not get the native grass. Before we reached Bannack the last tick had been emptied and we were sleeping on the hard boards of the wagon-bed. I chill when I think of those nights of watching, and the heavy mist that came just before the break-o'-day, shutting from view the bright stars, and spreading its gray mantle over the slumbering earth. It was damp and frosty. Trees and rocks sparkled like crystals, while the blue-green sage-brush was like waves of silver spangles."

I watched him closely as he spoke. There was an exquisite refinement beneath that rough exterior, and the picture he gave was beautiful.

"It was a strain every moment of the night," he said quietly, looking down, "and I was glad to see the morning star dim, and feel the air grow balmy as the crimson rays of the rising sun appeared. Those were anxious, but happy days. The buffalo and antelope wandered at will. We could kill prairie chickens, grouse and sage hens with a stick.

"When we reached Bannack our trying days came, for the camp and surrounding country were cursed with a lawless gang of robbers and murderers who spent their time in gambling and licentiousness of the vilest description. Lewd women from the slums of Eastern cities were brought into the community, and their resorts were hell-holes where many men were entrapped, robbed and murdered."

"Those certainly must have been stirring times," I interrupted.

"Yes," he continued. "Men who frequented the dance-houses for recreation were relieved of every dollar they took there, and those who expressed themselves as opposed to the bagnios and revolting horrors were shot, or in other manner murdered by unknown persons.

"As the days passed the ruffian power increased until it became absolutely necessary to take action. We were face to face with a dreadful issue, and at last the better element arranged for a secret meeting to be held at my father's home. This meeting of strong and pure-hearted men took place just before dawn one cold winter night, that hour being chosen as it was a time when fewer people were astir. The men came one or two at a time so as not to arouse suspicion for that might mean death.

"At the meeting we discussed the situation and the question, 'Have we the right to condemn to death a fellow man?' The decision we came to was, 'Yes, we have the right to protect our wives, daughters, property and ourselves against the worthless element.' We felt it a duty, in the absence of the law, to become a 'Court of Justice,' to handle the question. We realized we were face to face with an organized body of murderers, men and women saturated with social vice of the most repugnant nature.

"When a criminal was found in the community he was quietly taken away and given a trial. If death was the sentence he was quickly hanged. If the sentence was banishment, he was taken a few miles away and told to go, and he never came back, for he knew to return meant death. A suspicious character was warned to leave by placing 3-7-77 on his cabin door, or pinning the numbers on his pillow; 3 meant a grave three feet wide, 7 the number of feet long, and 77 inches deep.

THE FIRST VIGILANTE NOTICE OF MEETING

"It was not long after the organization of the Vigilantes that peace and security came to the people, and a lock was seldom found on a door, for robbery became almost unknown.

"Then for a while came happy days. In winter time the firelight danced cheerfully in our little log cabin home, casting fantastic reflections on the whitewashed walls; and in summer time soft perfume of wild flowers filled that same room where little tots played with rag dolls. Oh, how I loved that life! Our home was filled with love—the exquisite old-fashioned love we see so little of these days.

"A few years after peace and quiet came to us our happiness was marred by my mother's passing away. One day not long before death came I was alone with her. It was then she asked me not to become polygamous. This was not difficult for me to promise, for I had no intention of taking another wife. Not long after her funeral my father began preparations for a pilgrimage to Salt Lake. Then a break came between us, for he wished me to take another wife."

The old man left his chair and walked to a window where he stood for a few moments; then turning to me, said: "Come, it's a beautiful moonlight night; let us take a walk. I will show you an old scantling down the street where many lynchings have taken place."

Soon after we had left the smoke-filled room, he turned to me again and said: "I do not often have an opportunity like this. I get lonesome, and hungry mentally. My wife has passed away and my children are all married, so there seems little else for me to do evenings but sit and listen to the clink of poker chips. When an intelligent 'tenderfoot' comes along, I enjoy talking to him."

He smiled as he looked up to the clear moon. "It is such a wonderfully bright night, perhaps we shall hear a Montana nightingale sing before we return."

We had gone but a few yards when he stopped suddenly. "Listen," he said. "There it is now."

It was the mournful howl of a coyote. On the brow of a nearby hill, in fine silhouette, stood the timid animal with head uplifted to the moon—the guardian of the night.

"The time they seem to be bravest," he said, "is when the moon shines brightest. Whether or not the mournful wail is a supplication, human mind has never been able to tell."

He stopped as we turned a corner. "I would like to show you the spot near Bannack where we executed 'Dutch John' and several others," he said, "but perhaps this will interest you as much. The biggest lynching that was ever pulled off in the Territory was near here, but the first was in Bannack.

"In early days," he continued, "this street leading into the gulch was lined with hurdy-gurdies, gambling-houses, bagnios, and other hell-holes that seemed necessary to the happiness of the free-rangers of the hills. Road-agents, thieves, murderers and robbers congregated here."

We walked on in silence. Soon he stopped and turned to me: "Right here, one night, five road-agents were strung up. In full view of a crowd of people, five ropes were swung over a beam you see here, a noose was made at one end of each rope and left to dangle over an empty barrel or box."

"Were you one of the executioners?" I asked.

He made no reply to my question but continued: "All but one professed to have some religion in his makeup, a something that had been asleep for years, but suddenly came from the dormant state and manifested itself, for on the way from the courtroom to the place of hanging, one of them turned to one of the judges who walked close by, and said in all earnestness, 'Will you pray for me?' The procession halted and the judge dropped on his knees with 'Clubfoot George' kneeling on one side and Jack Gallagher on the other, and there offered up a fervent prayer for the welfare of the souls of the condemned road-agents, and then the procession moved on to the scaffold. When they reached the spot the condemned men were lined up, five in a row, some on boxes, some on upturned barrels. After the nooses were adjusted they were asked if they had any requests to make. 'If you have, they will be heeded,' said the chief judge.

" 'I want one more drink of whiskey before I die,' was Gallagher's last request, while Lyons begged to see his mistress. Gallagher's request sort of stunned some, and an old-timer called in a loud voice: 'We told 'em that we'd grant their request, so give 'im a drink.'

"He was given a generous 'shot'—a water-glass nearly full, and drained it to the last drop, refusing a 'chaser.'

" 'Clubfoot George' was the first to drop. When Gallagher saw his companion swing, he called out to the throng of onlookers: 'I hope I shall meet you all in the hottest pit in hell.' The words had hardly left his lips when the barrel he was standing on was pulled from underneath his feet.

" 'Kick away, old pard' called one of the others, as the body swayed, 'I'll meet you in hell in a short time.'

"After the last criminal had paid the penalty the bodies were left hanging for some hours and then turned over to friends if the unfortunates had any."

"And I would be willing to wager every one had at least one friend," I suggested. "I do not believe the person lives who can honestly say, 'I haven't a friend,' and I do not believe there is a person living who hasn't some good in him. There is a grave by a roadside in the northern part of the state. It is the lone grave of a woman. An old weather-beaten fence is built around the spot. There is no marker to tell whose body rests there. Old-timers who know hesitate to tell; still she had one friend at least, for at Christmas season a wreath is placed on a picket at one corner of the fence surrounding the grave. Stage passengers who ask are told it is a grave, that is all."

"Guess you are right," he said, as we turned from the scene of the tragedy and slowly started back towards the hotel. He was the first to break the silence, and spoke twice before getting my attention.

"Why so pensive?" he asked.

"I was thinking of Jack Gallagher's last request," I answered, and of an early morning back in Iowa when I was a young boy."

"Tell me about it," he said, with much interest. "It is now far past midnight; your stage leaves for Butte at daybreak; suppose we talk instead of sleeping."

I was glad to acquiesce, for I knew, should I go to bed, I might coax slumber in vain. I had a mental picture of Gallagher taking that large drink of whiskey just before going to the life beyond, and memory came to me of a still beside a river back East and men loading whiskey for Montana, and I could see two little boys in white night-gowns sitting on a fence watching men brand cattle to go with the whiskey, and I felt as if I were a partner in the deal.

"If you say you will stay up I shall feel greatly indebted to you," he said, "and you can tell me why you were thinking of that last request."

We had reached the hotel and taken chairs outside, as there was an all-night game on in the office and the players would have been disturbed by our voices.

"Now tell me why you were upset over that last request of Gallagher's," he said, as he moved his chair close to mine.

"I do not know why it should have upset me, but it did and I felt guilty," I answered slowly. "My uncle's first big stake was made by bringing whiskey into Montana from our Iowa home. Now as I look back and see the men rolling barrels from the mouth of a tunnel where they had been stored since the beginning of the Civil War, I feel that in some way we were associated with the criminals. Who knows but what some of that whiskey helped to make them criminals."

"Are you a prohibitionist?" he asked seriously.

"No," I answered, "but I am strong for high license. High enough to do away with the grogshop."

"I knew your uncle," he interrupted, "and I remember when he brought the whiskey into the Territory by 'bull-team.' He also was much interested in the Vigilante game, and if I am not mistaken, that is how he acquired the title of 'Judge.' " he laughed, in a teasing manner.

"Yes, I know that," I said, and I told how my brother and I, early one morning, crawled up on an old board fence and watched men brand cattle to drive overland with that 'bull-team.'

"Did you ever go back to the old home?"

"Yes," I said, and I thought how I had always regretted it. The childhood picture of my old home was that of a big, white house on a high hill; a house whose red roof dominated the whole landscape; a house whose windows looked down over a wide basin, and over a wonderful meadow, across a torrent river to a city with a background of wooded bluff. My longing to see the old home was great, so after many years I went back to the place. Then my happy dream faded away. The big house wasn't large. The hill was a rise of ground. The wonderful meadow was an ordinary field, and the wide, roaring torrent a placid stream. Iowaville, the city of my dream, stood near the river; a store or two near grimy houses leaning awry, their broken windows staring out over farm lands. The schoolhouse, where children once woke the echoes, was tumbling into ruin. Fences were gone and tangles of brush and briar hid unsightly ruins that had yielded to the tooth of time. Now and then a lonesome dog-bark was heard, and I was glad to get away.

"The reason I asked the question," said my old friend, "was that I was going to suggest to you not to go back. Things are never the same. People change. We change. Different environments change us. Our trend of thought changes, and it is always a disappointment. It is better to keep the old picture."

While talking we had not noticed the approach of dawn.

Chapter Two

FROM VIRGINIA CITY TO BUTTE

My mind was crowded with recollections as I took a seat beside the driver of the coach. It was a bright, crisp morning. Deep shadows were fading as the sun's crimson glow mounted higher and higher into the heavens, kissing the snow-white peaks which were like sails on a great, purple sea, for the clouds hung low. Soon we were passing down the main street behind four prancing horses and wheeled into Alder gulch headed for Butte.

Under a canopy of azure blue the scene had lost the mysteriousness of the evening before, and a spirit of life filled the air. Wild flowers that grew near the verdure-lined brook singing on its way to the valley below opened their petals and sent forth perfume. Birds saluted with their songs the new and balmy day, and life seemed, oh, so full.

I sat quietly drinking in the cool mountain air and feasting on the rugged scenery. The driver was the first to speak.

"I see you are a lover of nature," he said. "We are now passing over the first placer diggings of the state," he continued. "Up in Gold Creek the first nugget was found, but this was the first real 'diggings' where the cradle was used. This road follows a trail that was blazed many years ago by the red man who lived the healthy, free life of the open long before the pale-face came, bringing the vices of the East."

"I suppose that is what changed the whole story of his race," I interrupted, "from romance and poetry to squalor and poverty. In miserable camps on the outskirts of towns they hover near slaughter houses, some of the band gathering refuse while others sell polished horn and beadwork."

"I can tell you have been in Butte," he said quickly, as he touched up one of the leaders who was lagging.

As we approached the valley, mauve mist was rising and the scene was like a beautifully fascinating estuary. In the bright morning sun the view that lay before us was a kaleidoscopic joy. As we left the canyon the scene changed—so different but just as interesting, for it was a glint of the range-rider.

On the range that sloped down to the valley, hundreds of cattle were herded by picturesque cowboys, some silhouetted against the opalescent sky as the cattle fed on wild grass that grew on a rise of ground and as we rode on a breath of perfume came to us from the larkspur and sage brush.

At Sheridan I stopped off for two days and then took a ramshackle stage for Butte. We crossed the Continental Divide, and at the mouth of Nine Mile Canyon stopped at a road-house, a place to which in those days Butte people drove for recreation. A place where the society woman and queens of the "red-light" sat side by side as they shuffled their cards, where the man-of-affairs and a "secretary" from the underworld stood in pleasant intercourse while watching the marble ball of the roulette table.

We watched a game of faro for a few moments, and then passed on to the barren stretch that led to Butte. What seemed to be a low-hanging cloud hid the camp from view. Only a few mine stacks on the brow of the hill could be seen.

To accommodate a passenger who wished to go to a cabin near Timber Butte (a hill where one lone tree grew amongst granite boulders, thus giving the butte its name), the driver turned his horses into a road leading past a Cree Indian camp, the city dump, a slaughter house and four cemeteries huddled together. The Indians we passed were remnants of a brilliant and picturesque tribe of warriors, now forlorn wanderers waiting the call to the "Happy Hunting Ground."

Not far from along towards the city, ore was being roasted outside in the grounds of a reduction works, the fumes rising in clouds of cobalt blue, fading into gray, as it settled over the town like a pall. Indians called the dumps of burning ore "stink piles."

The driver reined in his horses as we entered the cloud of stifling sulphur and cautiously guided them up the hill. A policeman, with a sponge over his mouth and nose, to protect him from the fumes, led us to a little hotel in Broadway, for we could not see across a street. Lanterns and torches were carried by some to light the way through the sulphur cloud.

I was tired after the long ride, and before going to my room for the night, asked a tall, thin hack-driver who sat alone in the little office of the hotel if there was such a thing in town as a Turkish Bath.

"Oh, yes," he replied, "a fine one."

I asked him to direct me to it. It was in a basement at the corner of a street not far from the hotel. I walked to the place and passed down the steps into a room that was used as office and barber shop. An attendant showed me to a dressing room. While disrobing, I heard loud talking and laughter, both male and female voices. I paid little attention at the time, but when the attendant returned to take me to the bath, I spoke to him about it.

"Sure!" he said. "We've got a 'swell' bunch tonight."

"Do men and women go in together?" I asked.

"Sure! Come in and meet some of the ladies," he said, as he opened the door.

I asked him if they did not have private baths.

"Sure!" he replied seriously, sizing me up. "Ye ain't skeered, are ye?"

"No," I said, "but I do not wish to meet strangers tonight."

He showed me to a private bath and as he closed the door, I heard him say to a man who stood in the narrow passageway: "Another 'tenderfoot' in town."

Chapter Three

THE STRANGER'S FIRST GLIMPSE OF BUTTE

The Easterner's first impression of Butte as he enters the city is of horror by day and joy by night. There is tragedy and romance in the very look of the place and one's breath comes quickly. The barren granite boulders of the richest hill in the world are terrifying in the sunlight, but as eventide comes on tears often dim the stranger's eyes, for somberness comes with the purple tinge that settles over the scene. The three railroads that enter from the East pass through tunnels in the Continental Divide—a picturesque range of the Rockies—for the city lies just over the Divide on the Pacific slope. One road, after leaving its tunnel, skirts the side of the Highlands rising above Nine Mile Canyon. As the train reaches the valley it passes the desolate cemeteries, then over the girders that span a slag-walled creek; on over tailing dumps to a trestle where Frank Little was lynched, then into the station.

Another road passes through canyons where, in the spring, the walls are bowers of wild rose and forget-me-not. In the rockeries many varieties of wild flowers bloom, and clear, cool water sparkles and sings as it dances over the stones.

The train enters a tunnel, emerging in a few moments, and the passengers see below the only smelter left in the barren valley. The contrast is so startling they hold their breath. "It's more like hell than anything I had ever dreamed of," I heard a passenger say. Most of them sit spell-bound as the train quietly moves down the track leading past mines, through cuts in tailing dumps and past precipitating tanks on its way to the station.

The other train from a valley on the Atlantic slope laboriously winds its way up the mountain side, and as it emerges from a dripping granite-walled tunnel the passengers see before them another valley on the Pacific slope, dotted here and there with road-houses where society and the demi-monde join hands in revelry. At eventide, when mist settles over the valley, and lights are on, these places look like phantom ships sailing on a gray-purple sea. When the passenger approaches the city at night, the impression is wholly different, and he exclaims with joy, for the eye sees nothing but beauty.

Let us start from Jefferson Valley and climb the range called the Continental Divide.

> We will climb the rising hills
> Where the stately pine trees grow
> Towering o'er the sparkling rills
> That seek the valleys far below.
>
> There we'll tramp to nature's music
> While her beauty all beguiles—
> Tramp from mystic dusk-wrapped valley
> Through the green forest aisles.

Till at last the gray mist spreading
With the shades of eventide
See us standing there together
On the mighty Great Divide.

While the beauty of the sunset,
Like a tired child sunk to rest,
To the music of all nature
Now is fading from the West.

While on the mountainside to northward
Butte, her thousand lights ablaze
Like a pall of brilliant jewels,
Bursts upon the watcher's gaze.

Cloaked by night a thing of beauty,
Though ugly in the light of day,
Yet even so her odd fascination
Calls back her sons who go away.

One thing in the city sunlight and darkness does not change, and that is "Fat Jack," the hack driver, Butte's most picturesque character. He met the first train that came into the city, and meets them all, day and night. His silk hat looms above the other drivers as he quietly says to the traveler, "A carriage uptown?" From the beginning of railroads into Butte, he has been the one chosen to draw up the hill all celebrities visiting the camp. When President Roosevelt visited Montana the last time, it was "Fat Jack" who met him at the station. When the Colonel came down the steps of his car he waved his hand, and called "Hello, Jack!" for the Colonel never forgot and they were friends in early days.

Chapter Four

WANDERING AROUND

One night a friend came to me and said: "How would you like to go to the theater, and after that just wander around a little and take in some of the sights?" I was a stranger in town at the time and was glad of the opportunity.

We started out and turned into Main Street and on down the hill. In front of a building with a sign over the door, "The Comique," a crowd was standing on the sidewalk. He turned to me and said: "We'll go around in the alley and enter that way; that's where the respectable people go in."

We went to the next street below and walked on until we came to an alley. Not far up the passageway was a light hanging over a door. He opened the door and we passed up a narrow flight of stairs leading to the "gallery," as it was called. In reality, it was a circle of stall-like boxes, each place a compartment with a bolt on the inside of the door and a small slide where drinks were passed in.

AN INDIAN WRESTLER

The front of the box—as it was called—that looked down upon the stage and floor below was enclosed by a wire netting. A scene was painted on this screen, the effect being that the occupants of the compartment could see all that was going on and not be seen from floor or stage.

On the floor below sawdust was sprinkled. Tables for four were here and there about the auditorium. Girls in gaudy evening dress were waitresses and entertainers. At intervals one would mount a table and do a terpsichorean stunt, much to the amusement of the loungers.

The performance on the stage was on the order of our present-day vaudeville, with a few extras to suit the occasion. An encore was the signal for boisterous applause and the throwing of coins at the artist. Many a coin went which might otherwise have gone to buy a loaf of bread for a hungry child, or helped to pay for a gown for a deserving wife.

We had been there but a short time when my friend said: "Please excuse me for a moment; I hear a familiar voice in the next box."

In a few moments he returned. "We're invited in next door," he said, with an amused smile.

We went in. There were two occupants of the box: my landlord and a painted beauty seated on his lap. Soon a tray with drinks on was passed through the slide. A small red ticket was on the tray, and the painted beauty quickly reached out her hand and took the bit of cardboard and put it in her stocking. It represented her commission.

We stayed but a short time in this place and then went out into the fresh air. We turned into a street running east and west. It seemed like a street leading into hell, and parts of it would cause one to close one's eyes. Many men and boys were idly passing along the sidewalk. Young men, splendidly receptive, and beautifully unthinking boys, were there just wandering about. Chinamen, with wash-basket on the shoulder, hurried down the walk, while the silent Indian with gay-colored blanket wrapped closely around his body passed quietly along, looking upon a scene in which his people took no part.

We walked slowly along this thoroughfare of the underworld, stopping here and there to make observations. Loud music from the dance halls filled the air. Now and then click-click-click was heard: the rattle of the red, white and blue ivory chips of a poker game; innocent looking things, but tragic, for many represented the day's wage of a toiler who was too weak to withstand the temptation of the bright lights.

From beginning to end the street was emerged in emotion: here careless joy, there sad. On either side were one-story shacks, a door and one window in front, the name of the occupant of the "crib" either in gaudy letters over the door or white showing through ruby-colored glass in window or transom.

Blondetta stood in her doorway. Many peroxide puffs adorned her head; her cheap, showy dress was cut low at the neck; no sleeves to cover her large, flabby arms; the skirt came down to the knees.

Her neighbor, puffing a cigarette, leaned lazily out of her window; her painted face showed the lines of a hard life. The strollers usually passed her by and stopped for a chat with French Erma. They nevertheless received the stereotyped greeting: "Hello, boys!" Then the eyes of the "dope fiend" would almost close and at times it seemed as if she were about to fall asleep. A footstep would rouse her for a moment and the passer-by would hear the weird voice: "Hello, boys!" Some would stop a moment and then pass on to a more attractive shack. Once in a while an old-timer who had known her in her palmy days would reach in his pocket and pull out a few silver pieces and hand them to her with the cold words: "Here, Carmen, go buy yourself a drink." Her long, bony hand would reach out for the coins and her painted lips form an invitation to the old-time friend: "Won't you come in and have a drink with me?" "No," was most always the answer, as he passed on to another "crib."

I felt that the old fiend, as she stood in the realm of shadows and took the occasional carelessly-flung bit of silver, mourned over the ingratitude and falling away of a friend in whom she once deemed she could confide, as with ever-increasing force the barrenness of the empty years forced itself even upon her dull consciousness—just another bit of tribute of flesh and blood that the pitiless city exacted.

Not far along the walk in another "crib" "Jew Jess" sat rocking near her open door. She was talking with "Micky, the Greek," who stood near. The little one-room cabin looked neat, and an air of an humble home seemed to surround the place. A bed in one corner; in another a stove just large enough for a tea-kettle to sit on the top. A few pictures hung on the wall, and on a shelf adorned with festoons of home-made lace there were several photographs arranged artistically. While rocking and talking her fingers were busy with knitting needles.

I do not believe, after all, any of those women were there of their own volition. Some tragedy sent them there.

> Some one who greeted her eye in the smile of a
>   friend,
> In a voice intended to sway;
> Some one who cared not for the bitter end,
> Or the part his act might play.

Typical of Butte, these little "cribs" were owned by influential people and rented to the unfortunates for one dollar a night—rent paid in advance, for respectability best of all knows how great a tribute to exact from the unfortunates.

Some ten years ago a moral wave passed over the city, and the front doors and windows of these places were boarded up. Sidewalks were laid in the alleys. Beacon lights were hung here and there to guide men and boys to the passageways where the inmates solicited from the rear door.

Boarding up the front doors and windows of the "crib" in the underworld and opening the back gave more latitude for crime. The reformers were satisfied. The city was not deprived of its revenue, the respectable of their rents, nor the policemen of their graft.

In later years an ex-official told me how the unfortunates were held up on every turn. He said, "There is a state law prohibiting such places, but the city evaded it. Once a month warrants were issued for the arrest of these women. The warrants were served," he continued; "some of them would go up to headquarters and pay a fine of ten dollars. Three receipts were issued; one for the Chief, one for the city and one for the woman. Some did not go up, and in that case an officer would call on her and collect the ten dollars and give her a receipt that had been made out at headquarters."

He said the policeman on the beat also had his graft. "They walked along," he said, "and if nobody was looking, he would stick his head in the window or door and tell the inmate to lay a few dollars out of sight on the window sill where he could get it when he came back and she knew what would happen if she did not comply."

On our way back to my hotel we stopped at the Casino just as "Fat Jack" drove up with a "slumming party." They were from Butte's exclusive set, and occupied a box directly opposite the one in which we sat. They seemed to think it was more romantic or sporty to have Jack drive upon such occasions. The place was an "underworld" dance hall with cheap vaudeville. After each act the patrons of the place would adjourn to the dance hall. Here, at one end, was a long bar where men and women after each dance lined up for drinks. I watched the members of this "slumming party" as the night wore on and they became riper and riper after each dance, until at last all classes and conditions joined hands in "high-jinks" of the liveliest character. The seductive drink softened the veneer, and it fell away, leaving them in their natural state, and the world outside was forgotten.

Finally the restricted district was done away with. At the present time another reform movement is on and some reformers suggest that the section be re-established as a protection to the home and the young people growing up, for now it is a case of "Who's your neighbor?"

Chapter Five

"DOPE" COLONY

I was standing on the edge of the sidewalk one night
opposite a hotel where, from the balcony, Roosevelt was
addressing the people who thronged the street. A young
man joined me and presented a card. He was a writer for a
New York publication. What he handed me was a card of
introduction from Colonel Roosevelt. He had come as far
as Butte with the Colonel's party and was going to stop in
the city for a few days to gather data for his publication. It
was a pleasure to meet him, for in this part of the world
where one gets so few thoughts that are not commercial, it
is refreshing to come across a genius, and I cordially
welcomed him.

He remarked that he had read my story of the "Snowbird,"
and wished first to see that section of the city. The
following night, therefore, not long after dinner, we started
out. I first took him to a drug-store where the proprietor
told me his revenue from the sale of morphine alone was
between five and six hundred dollars a month.

When we reached the place it was about the time the "hop-heads," as they are called, begin to come for the narcotic. We sat where we could see them as they came in and walked to the rear of the store where a clerk waited on them. Packages for the regular customers were already done up. They received their "dope," paid the clerk, and silently walked out. "Callahan the Bum" was the first to come, and then a "fiend" arrived, who always had four dogs following him. As he came in, the proprietor said to us: "That fellow buys quite a lot; a prominent citizen gives him the money, he gets the 'dope,' and they divide."

We left the place shortly and went to a fruit store where I bought a basket of fruit, then with my companion walked to Arizona street, where we turned and went south until we came to a little shack that stood at the corner of a street leading into the section we were headed for. An old woman addicted to the drug habit lived in here. The yard was filled with rubbish consisting of empty cans and bits of iron gathered by her from around town to sell to those in charge of precipitating plants.

"Butte certainly is a place of strong contrasts," said the stranger. "I notice mine shafts in back and front yards, and one stands on a corner opposite my hotel."

"Yes," I replied, "and children play on decomposed granite where cows lie chewing their cud. We have the extremes— the best and the worst in the world."

"Tell me," he said, as he turned and pointed to a tall, thin man who wore a silk hat and a light brown uniform with brass buttons, "who is that odd-looking fellow? I know he is a hack driver, for he drove the hack the President rode in, and how frightfully thin he is." "Yes," I smiled, "that is, of course, the reason he has been given the nickname 'Fat Jack.' That fellow is known all over the country from the

Atlantic to the Pacific; and has been the subject for many a 'write-up.' "

We now turned into a narrow winding street, almost an alley. No sidewalks were laid through this section of the city. My friend asked if these cabins were built by the people now occupying them. I told him they were built by miners of early days—days of the placer diggings.

"A little later," I said, "after we have investigated some of them and discussed certain of the inmates we will go over to the original diggings where prospectors looked only for gold. In these tumbled-down shacks the very air we breathe whispers of tragedy."

Society would seem to recognize no duties towards the dwellers in the cabins, but society in Butte is little different from anywhere else. The many follow the leader. They are not sure of themselves. Should some one of prominence start to do something for the poor wretches here, it would at once become a fad and the section would be overrun by hypocrites.

We now neared the cabin of a one-time society leader of another city. "First," I said, taking him by the arm, "I will take you to a cabin just around the corner where I want to leave this fruit. I know the life-story of the poor woman who occupies the hovel. To most people she is merely a woman of mystery. One day she told me of the tragedy that had entered her life. It was at a time when she lay desperately sick with no one to care for her. At that time she thought death was near. The poor little withered-up body is all you will see of a once beautiful woman. She may have several friends with her, victims, of course, of the narcotic, for they hover together and tell marvelous and weird tales, not unlike those of the absinthe 'fiend,' but not as cowardly. The latter is possessed with pitiful fear and one can drive him with a wave of the hand. I studied those poor wretches at Montmartre while gathering material for a write-up."

"I should like to hear these people talk," he said as we neared the door. In replying, I reminded him that in cases of the drug habit the brain becomes so thoroughly poisoned and abnormal that the victims imagine most wonderful things. They lose all moral sense. If they have a friend who is not addicted to the habit they are not happy until they make a "fiend" of that friend. To take the drug from them makes them criminals of the most desperate type, since they will do anything to get the narcotic. Some of these unfortunates take as high as fifty grains of morphine a day. One grain would be dangerous for a normal person. One-half a grain is a strenuous dose.

"Tell me of the life of this one here," he said.

"After we have been inside I will tell you the story of her life. I do not wish to do it now, for I want to see if you can give a correct guess as to her former life, and whether or not she is of high or low birth. Do not be surprised at her friendliness towards me. She is grateful for some small services I have been able to do for her."

I pushed open the door without stopping to knock. The cabin had settled and the door was out of plumb and could not be locked. There seemed at first to be no life in the one-room shack, but as our eyes became accustomed to the dim light of one candle burning low, we saw lying on the bed two seemingly lifeless women. On the floor near an old wreck of a stove lay a man with his head resting on a roll of rags. In his right hand which had fallen away from his body was clutched an opium pipe.

"We will not rouse them," I said. "If awakened now they would be sluggish and repulsive. They have had their early night's 'shot' and will be dead to the world for hours."

"This little woman lying here," I said, as we moved closer to the bed, "is the one I told you about. Take particular notice of her companion and I will tell you of them both when we go out."

He did not speak as he stepped nearer the dilapidated bed where lay the two stupefied figures. The picture of wretchedness was too much for him and he quickly turned away.

"Come, let us get out of here," he whispered, as he hurried to the door and out into the fresh air of the narrow street.

We sat for some time on an upturned box near the side of the cabin, while I told him something of the history of the unfortunates we had seen.

Of the two women my little friend had been the stronger character. I say "my little friend," for I have always felt a deep and real sympathy for her in her great sorrow; she tried hard at first to make good. She told me the drug held her in its grasp like the coils of a snake, and when the craving was on she was as helpless as a babe. One day when I went to see her, her sad little face looked up to mine as she said: "I cannot give it up. The prick of the needle is the pleasantest sensation of my life. Go away and do not try and influence me. It is all the comfort I have in the world."

Both were society women. Reverses came to them about the same time, and it was not long before invitations became few and far between, and soon they were only "memories." The little woman bore up like a soldier for a

long, long time. The husband gave way first to drink—
then drugs, and, unknown to her, administered morphine
to her in medicine. She made the discovery when it was
too late.

My companion inquired how the drug was taken.

"Usually whiskey and morphine first," I answered, "and
when the exchequer gets low they resort to cheaper drugs,
such as cocaine and opium. Cocaine 'fiends' are called
'snow-birds,' for they put some of the white powder on
the back of the hand and then sniff it into the nose.
Morphine is sometimes prepared in a substance that
resembles a mint wafer and 'fiends' are often seen chewing
them while standing around the street. Men are perhaps
more prone to 'hit' the opium pipe, but I have seen in the
Mott Street section of New York City men and women—
white, brown and yellow—lounging together in one room,
all enjoying the sensation of the pipe."

"That other woman," I continued, "was handsome,
restless and susceptible to the suave words of man. After
her husband's death, a coward broke her life and made her
what she is. She was ambitious and believed the promises
he made to her.

"This fellow knew she was not strong enough mentally to
battle with financial reverses. He wound his coils around
her, and she soon became his mistress and from day to day
sank lower. He tired of her and deserted her; she then
quickly drifted down."

In another cabin visited that evening on our walk, we saw
an unusual character. I knew her years ago in a western
city; she was then a leader in social and other affairs, and at
the opening of an opera house she was one of a theater
party I attended. The party was given by an editor-in-chief

of a leading news-paper. Years after I came down to the cabin we have just left. The little woman we have seen was desperately sick with pneumonia and I had come to see what I could do for her. Another woman, seemingly a stranger to me, was there—blear-eyed and dopey. There seemed to be something familiar about her—a something I had seen before. As she sat in the little cabin I studied her interesting face. Even in that condition her conversation was colored with aphorism. I think what first interested me most and caused me to study her more closely was the relic of a one-time beautiful gown she was wearing and the artistic arrangement of her hair. Bit by bit recognition came to me and I was staggered.

I did not let her know I recognized her until later when I went to her cabin to try and find out what had brought her to that end. At first she strenuously denied her identity, but when she found it was of no use, the scene was most pitiful. In her day she had been beautiful, talented, and with a charm of manner possessed by few. Flattery ruined her, and the home was neglected. What a home she could have made for a group of little tots: a life of love, happiness, ease and content. Flattery blinded her and led her on a chase for the thing she thought would bring happiness. In a manner she attained the thing she looked for, but like the fabled apple of Hesperides, it turned to ashes on her lips. It ruined the home and she drifted to the shadows, and now she is what we find her today: a helpless "dope fiend," and the people in the other part of town close their eyes to this section.

The tendency in fact is to kick these unfortunates a little lower. I have been criticized severely by some eminently respectable people for coming here and helping them in small ways. The day I went to see this woman she implored me to write to her husband and ask him to come to her and close all the gates of grief. I did as she requested, and in about one week's time a reply to my letter came. It told of his death. As I read the letter to her I watched her expression change and my mind traveled back to Rock Creek cemetery near Washington, D.C., where an unknown grave is marked by a statue by Saint Gaudens, called "Grief."

It is the figure of a beautiful woman with a face that haunts one. With her chin resting on her hand, she gazes into space with the longing, appealing look of one who has suffered much. The expression of the face but reveals more vividly the look of the eyes, and there she sits day and night, year in and year out, looking for the thing she lost, waiting its return. It passed her once: she did not realize it was going away. It has called her the last time.

"Come, let us go in for a few moments," suggested the writer.

We stayed and talked for some time with the unfortunate woman. When we came out he said, as he slowly shook his head: "That scene presents as complete a tragedy as has ever been written by any of the playwrights of modem times."

"Yes," I said, "the play is nearly ended and the actress will soon be going out into the night. The poor woman has drifted beyond help, broken in health, with heart scars that will never heal. In the still, small hours when she is alone and without 'dope' they ache and ache, and years cannot heal the pain which is her constant companion. Soon she will sleep beneath a shroud of tansy weed and the board at the head of her grave will be marked 'Unknown' "

As we walked on I suggested we had better leave the diggings for a daylight trip and go to Chinatown instead, as it was on our way back to the hotel. "I want you to go to the Mission where I often go and play for them to sing," I said.

The Mission was open when we reached it and a number of Chinamen were idly sitting about. They were glad to see us, for it meant a song for them. One said to me as we went in: "Mister George, he velly kind; he come and play for us to sling."

They gathered around the old squeaky organ and sang for about an hour, their preference being for gospel hymns. While the others were singing, one, unobserved by either myself or my friend, went quietly out and returned with a present for the writer, an act of courtesy characteristic of the Chinese.

"I should think you would be unhappy in this environment."

"No," I answered, "I am glad to be here and in my small way help some wandering soul. It is not necessary to rush to the big cities to find work to do. Here in this far western city one can, if he will, make some wretched soul feel that there are days of spring, and the dewdrops still sparkle in the hearts of flowers."

"I think you are right," he said. "How splendid it is to feel we give to the world a pleasant thought, rather than take away."

We had reached the hotel and stopped as we heard the screeching sound of wheels. It was an ore train on its way through the main streets of the city to a smelter in the valley, turning the corner where the hotel stood.

Chapter Six

CEMETERIES OF BUTTE

Some say a cemetery reflects the spirit of the people of the community. Let us hope that sometimes mistakes are made, for Butte cemeteries are desolate and have often been the subject for eastern writers. Graves cannot be dug on the hills, for they are mostly of solid rock. A section in the valley was chosen for the resting-place of the dead. It seems as if it had been the bed of a lake that had existed long before the white man came, for the wash of decomposed granite from the hills is like coarse sand and in it graves are easily dug. It is impregnated with mineral and unsuccessful attempts have been made by unfeeling placer prospectors to make locations in the desolate spot. Here are grouped the resting-places of the Chinese, Catholic, Jew and Protestants—I should make an exception for the Chinese, for at stated times the bodies that have been buried for a certain length of time are taken up and boiled so as to remove all flesh remaining on the bones, and when that is done the bones are packed in small boxes and shipped to China for final burial. Surrounding this cheerless spot is a brick-yard, two slaughter houses, the city dump, and a place where, in early days, ore was roasted in the open, and the fumes settled over the graves. Tansy weed was about all that would grow in the lonely spot. Weather-beaten crosses and board-markers were much in evidence, and many a tansy knoll told of a broken heart. Here and there this peculiar green shrouded a suicide's grave or that of an unknown. In early days disappointments that led to dissipation caused many to take their own lives, and many, unknown by name who had drifted West, sank under the weight of sorrows, and now sleep in this spot. As a rule frontier cemeteries are desolate, but I know of none more forsaken than the old cemeteries of Butte. I have seen in Alaska barren spots, but they did not seem to whisper of as great tragedy. In the Catholic cemetery, near a ravine where, in the Spring, water flows swiftly and washes much away, is a sad-looking section, for it is filled with tiny graves—graves of little tots who were blessed by early passing away. Two new cemeteries are on Butte's Appian Way that winds across the "Flat." It is like the way leading into Rome, for the two cemeteries are on one side of the way as the catacombs of the Italian city. We might draw on our imagination and see "Barney's" road-house as Saint Sebastian, and one a little farther beyond as the tomb of Saint Cecilia. Not long ago I walked through one of these cemeteries and did not see but two or three tombstones with American names engraved upon them, and the graves are rows of verdureless mounds.

Chapter Seven

MANY JOYS

Butte is barren but not shorn of all joys, and there are many beautiful spots surrounding this unique city. Columbia Gardens is one of these—restful and quiet, a wonderland of nature. The air is filled with soft music of whispering pines and the song of rippling water as it dances under rustic bridges and past verdure-lined paths and beds of bloom on its way to the valley below. It is not a canyon nor a hiatus, but more a miniature valley and benchland, where the perfume of wild flowers is everywhere and song birds carol amid the branches of Canadian Poplars and Balm of Gilead. In this spot grow the most beautiful pansies the world has ever known. Surrounded by a great profusion of flowers there is a miniature lake and a handsome dance pavilion.

The electric cars leave the noisy city and pass through a cut in a tailing dump, precipitating tanks where copper-impregnated water from the mines flows over bits of iron and tin cans that fill tanks, precipitating the copper that is in the water, and then past a smelter and on up a grade to the city's playground that nestles close to the mountains of the Continental Divide.

In this pretty park as we pass through arbored and bloom-lined walks, we come to a spot where the canyon air is cool and refreshing, and where the artistic fern lifts its head, where winds breathe low and waters softly ripple with a lullaby sound.

> It is in this spot where grows the stately fern
> I go with my love so pure and fair,
> As seeking rest from the barren city we turn
> To this quiet place in the canyon's care.

From a rustic bench in this sheltered spot we can see the moon rise three times. The mountain peaks behind the park give this effect. The moon comes up and passes behind a peak, then out for a few moments, then behind another, and out again and starts on its journey through the heavens.

> And at our feet is a placid pool
> Cool as the canyon's breath,
> Its waters sparkle like a wonderful jewel
> In the rays of the bright moondrift.

> The quiet spot is a place for trysting
> And where lovers give their plight,
> For the God of love is in the perfumed air,
> In the shadows, and bright moonlight.

COUNTRY LIFE OF THE AUTHOR

Lake Avoca is another pretty resort. A few years ago, a party of Finlanders were holding a picnic at the lake. One made a wager that he could dive and stay under the water longer than the other. The challenge was accepted. It was agreed upon that the parties to the contest were to row out to the middle of the lake and at a given signal dive from their boats. The signal was given and they went over the side. In a short time one came to the surface. Some moments passed but the other did not come up. When the rescuing crew brought the body to the surface it was found he had weights tied to his feet.

Funerals are a great source of joy to many. A young fellow hires a horse and buggy and with his girl follows the hearse until it turns into the cemetery, and then, as he comes to the gate, he whips up the horse and it hurries on over the "Flat" to the road-houses, where the rest of the day is spent in revelry. Hardly a night passes but what "Fat Jack" carries a party of "joy riders" to the "Flat."

It is over this "Flat" that one of Butte's old-timers used to go hunting the Jackrabbit. He had a one-horse vehicle and would put his small children in the bed of the wagon and start out for a day's sport. The horse would sight a rabbit dodging in and out of the sage-brush, and without warning to the driver, start pell-mell cross-country in pursuit of the game. Often a youngster would be jostled out and the horse travel on at break-neck speed for half a mile or so, before the father would discover the loss. He would turn and go back for the child, and then renew the chase. Those were days of real sport—happy days when the pumpkin pie was made with a brown paper crust.

It is a joy and great lark to the stranger to take a meal in the smallest restaurant in the world. It is a place between two buildings, and has seating capacity for six.

A young man, who had been a "mucker" in one of the Company mines, married and went to New York on his honeymoon, and while in that city he called on one of the high officials of the company. The official's family was away and he thought it would be a lark to take the young couple to his country home to stay over night. Men of large affairs often do such things when their wives are away from home. It is a change of trend of thought, and a provincial chap interests them. The official told me the story one day as we sat on the upper deck of the old steamship *Baltic*. We were headed for England and the sea was rough. He said with much mirth, "I took them aboard my yacht and we steamed down the sound to Fairhaven. That night they were shown to one of the guest chambers where were twin beds. I was going through the upper hall the morning after and met the housekeeper coming out of the apartment. She was smiling," he continued, "and motioned me to follow her as she passed back through the door; and when I went in I saw the occasion of mirth— only one of the beds had been occupied. There were not many twin beds in Butte in those days," he laughed, "and I suppose the young fellow lay awake most of the night wondering who was going to occupy the other bed."

One of the happiest homes in Butte is one where the first stones of the foundation were laid in a matrimonial bureau of an eastern city. The young bride-elect was shipped West C.O.D. It was years ago when I was on the *Herald*. Across the street from the newspaper building was a matrimonial agency. One night the head of the concern came to see me and said, "I have a splendid story." He told how he had that day shipped two young women to Montana C.O.D.

"One went to Miles City," he said, "and one to Butte." I asked him how that could be, and he told of having received these requests for wives after the senders had read his advertisements.

He said, "After the money for the traveling expenses and the fee of fifty dollars had been placed in the bank at Miles City and at Butte I bought their tickets and sent them on."

I remembered the names and after many years looked up the one that had been ticketed to Butte and found her a very happy and prosperous wife with an interesting family of children. After becoming pretty well acquainted with the husband, he told me how he had married his wife and the happy life they had led.

"At the time I lived far out in the country," he said, "and did not have an opportunity to meet young women and so resorted to the agency and have always been thankful I did—it's safer than society," he said with a serious smile.

Chapter Eight

FOREIGN POPULATION

Some years ago I was traveling on the Rhine in Germany, and one afternoon while sitting on the deck of my steamer enjoying the ever-changing scene, an Irishman came to where I sat and drew a chair close to mine, and as he took a seat beside me, he said in way of making conversation, "You are from the States?" "Yes," I answered, "I am from America." "What part?" he asked, with a truly Irish accent. "I am from Montana," I answered. "From Butte?" he asked quickly. When I told him I was he then mentioned the name of a priest, and asked me if I knew him. When I told him I did, he said, "He is my brother, and in a recent letter to my wife he wrote, 'Living in Butte is about like being in Ireland.'"

Authors visit Butte, write stories, and go away, but they do not get the true atmosphere. They come to a city of upwards of one hundred thousand inhabitants, and do not find a bookstore in the place.

One day I was walking along one of the business streets when a man opened the door of a store and called to me,

"Come in, I want to show you something." He pointed to the side wall of a store where toys, office furniture and stationery were sold. It was the wall opposite a soft-drink fountain. "Just think! Seven shelves of books in Butte," he said in much merriment. The proprietor of the place had put in a few books, and was uncertain as to the advisability of the venture.

There is a dry-goods store with three or four shelves of popular novels, and a branch of the Post Office where a news stand is in connection, a place where fashion-plates, pictorials, stationery and books are sold.

While making a report on the alien situation during the period of the war, I came in touch with forty-seven different nationalities, and during the sickness that followed I found I had overlooked five. There is the Finlander Hall. The Greeks, Turks, Austrians, and those of many other nationalities have their clubs, and in these meeting-places the native tongue is spoken, and they have literature from the Fatherland.

The stranger visiting Butte marvels at the attire of many of the young women on the streets, and the powdered faces and rouged lips of school girls. In most instances these young women and girls are not to blame. The blame lies with those who ought to set a good example, and who do not.

The foreigners who come to our shores by steerage are tagged at Ellis Island and distributed to different parts of the country. Those coming to Butte do not see or know anything of American life. They make a good wage, and naturally want to adopt American ways. The wooden shoe is laid aside for the French heel, and the dress is often daring, and they argue this way as they refer to the different society women, "It must be all right, for they do it and they ought to know." Those who adhere to their home custom are more picturesque and interesting. In the Italian sections where the bright colors of the South are used, the picture is fascinating, and helps to soften the harshness of the barren surroundings.

A striking character passing down the street is a Serbian priest as he leads a funeral procession. At one time I witnessed a Serbian funeral. It was after a mine disaster and there were five hearses in the procession. The priest in full vestments walked in front of the first hearse as if to lead the way of the souls of the departed.

The same day another funeral procession passed down the hill on its way to the valley, and in front of the hearse walked a young man and woman. The young woman was in white, and carried a wreath of flowers. At first glance, without seeing the hearse one would think it a wedding procession. Why the city looks so strange is the many different nationalities in the streets, and their homes suggest their native land and make a conglomeration of architecture.

Chapter Nine

EXTREMES IN SOCIETY

Once in awhile a few of the old set—the set that was instrumental in giving Butte its world-wide reputation for lavish entertainments, beautiful and beautifully-gowned women, and bright, dashing men—get together and travel down the "road to yesterday," but, oh! what a change they see. There are only a few of the old set left and no more sparkling society events for those of the old set who are left have stepped aside for the newcomers and are now merely onlookers. The whole atmosphere has changed from the brilliant to the mass. The person, no matter from what walk in life, who makes a "strike" is in it socially if he or she cares to be, for money counts absolutely. True friendship is little known. It is only an acquaintance with a motive "what can I gain by knowing him?"

There is so little mental companionship, and many are afraid to acknowledge friendship with a person who is not subservient to the powers that be.

Social deception and character assassination appeared at the beginning of the great copper war. People lined up on one side or the other, and the old-time good fellowship vanished and they would go the limit to injure a person morally or financially who did not champion their cause. They were abject slaves to one side or the other. The great battle is over, but the morale of the people is still upset.

In the early days, three establishments sent their modistes to Paris twice a year to buy gowns and select designs, and the Butte women—beautiful and attractive—gowned in the latest creations from the French metropolis, drew admiration wherever they went.

There were no prudes; no conventionality. Gambling houses were rented for a night for social entertainments, giving men and women a like opportunity to "buck the tiger."

One of the most talked of social affairs of those days was the opening of the "Irish World," the most exclusive resort in the restricted district. Engraved invitations were sent to the male gender of the "four hundred," and in most cases the R.S.V.P. was acknowledged by their presence, "Ladies" from other fashionable resorts were there, and some stood in the receiving line. Carriages lined the street and men in evening dress hurried in and out of the place. Often, on a pleasant day, the proprietress of this resort would be seen out for a drive on the principal streets of the city. She used to sit in an open landau surrounded by three or four of her leading "ladies." Her large diamond earrings blazed like the headlights of an engine. The beautiful women and bright colors of wonderful gowns, picture-hats and sparkling jewels made a picture that resembled a bouquet on wheels.

In a brief way let me give a pen picture of one or two social affairs given by prominent people. Two having taken place about the same time, or perhaps a week or ten days intervening, and of such a startling difference, perhaps it would be of more interest to write of them, and the impression made upon a stranger from one of the middle states who had read much of Butte and held a slight doubt as to the truth of some of the stories.

These two people I am to mention were numbered among Butte's best entertainers. In fact, others were mediocre in comparison.

This first function I am to speak of was given in one of the first substantial residences built in Butte. When fortune smiled upon the family, and the number of little ones increased, it was decided the cabin of frontier days was too small for their comfort and a new house was planned. The mother loved the old location, for it was where her happiest days were spent; so the old, much beloved cabin was supplanted by a commodious building. The home was ideal. The mother, a natural student, imparted much to the children, and her influence for good was felt amongst her myriad of friends, and as the summers passed, the sweeter she bloomed. She felt that a woman's soul should be pure like a white bird, unruffled and unsullied. At her home one found intellectual rest.

This night I was the escort of the visitor from Chicago. As the door of the homey house swung open, we were ushered to a stair leading to rooms above where removed our wraps. In a moment we were ready to go to the floor below. About halfway down the stairs we stopped to let our eyes travel over the brilliant scene and enjoy a breath of perfume from the fresh blossoms. The four matrons in the receiving line shone like that many stars. The jewels and rich-spangled gowns dazzled the stranger. We moved on a few steps. She took me by the arm as if to hold me back.

"It is more brilliant than anything I had dreamed of," she softly said, as her eyes traveled over the fascinating scene.

After we passed the receiving line, I spoke in undertone. "This is one of the few homes where money does not rule; where the atmosphere is honest and an invitation to the home means friendship in the true sense of the word. Our hostess is sure of her position and will not tolerate the yellow streak, and you know it always shows in one way or another."

"It is a beautiful reception," was all she said, as we moved on towards the library.

Soft notes from the orchestra came to us. We passed on into another room and were soon lost in the maze of dancers.

"There is so much beauty in life unseen in colors," she said quietly, as we passed around the room.

"Do you mean all this loveliness in our barren city?" I asked, as we left the room and found a cozy nook where we might see all and our tete-a-tete not be disturbed, "True, our city is barren and ugly to look at, but we have so much of the beautiful surrounding us to offset that. You should visit here at a time the foothills are turning green and the canyons bowers of wild roses. A time when small flowers lift their dainty heads from amongst blades of crisp grass and kiss the heavens with their perfume. Montana has a greater variety of wild flowers than any other state in the Union."

"Tell me," she asked, "about the dance your friend is going to give next week."

I smiled as I answered her. "He is a prince of entertainers; a man of dual nature. I wish this affair he is to give was to be one of his honest entertainments, but it is not to be. It is for business purposes only. He is in the big copper fight and out for big stakes, and playing the game for all there is in it. It is a case of 'dog eat dog,'" I said. "Both he and his antagonists have special agents everywhere. You probably are at this present time suspected of being here for some sinister motive."

She looked much surprised at my words. How is that?" she asked.

"Butte is a city of listeners," I said, "and you no doubt have been reported on long before this. If a man or woman comes to the camp and goes about his or her business, attending to his or her affairs only, he or she—whichever it may be—is looked upon with suspicion, suspected of gathering information to be used by one faction or another."

"A peculiar atmosphere to live in," she suggested.

"Yes," I said, "the city reminds me of an island far out at sea: it has individuality unique and interesting. At times I tire of the place and long for shores where the seagull calls. Where I can look out on the blue waters, where all is restful and quiet. Where I can expand my lungs and drink in the pure ozone. The affair next week will be quite a medley. In preparing the invitation list for such affairs, he calls in one or two of his attorneys. 'How about this fellow?' he may ask—or, 'Can we gain anything by asking him?' and so they go over the list. He has two distinct sides to his character. When he entertains for his friends only, it is most delightful. Where his enemies fail, is in a lack of knowledge."

"In other words," she smiled, "he out-generals them in both good and bad."

Chapter Ten

SOME INTERESTING CHARACTERS

Many people do not understand the significance of the term "squaw-man." In most instances, environments bring about the peculiar connubial state, but it is usually the renegade white man who marries a squaw merely to have some one to take care of him—gather the firewood—prepare the game and hides as he brings them in, but in most cases they lie around the camp and let the squaw do it all. They are much like another type of male who infests our country, and that is the foreigner who comes here in quest of a woman with money, or one physically or mentally qualified to take care of him.

Butte boasts, and has reason to be proud of the highest class "squaw-man" the country has ever known. In early days he loved and married a squaw. She bore his children and he was the devoted husband and father until night came to the mother and she fell asleep, while the curtain rang down and her soul started on its journey to the "happy hunting grounds." He educated his children. The daughter returned from an Eastern school and grieved herself to death, and the sons, excepting one, returned to the tepee. He then married a white woman, and later on was given the post of Ambassador to a foreign country. He was a scholar, and author, and recently, at a ripe old age, his tired body was laid to rest, and at his graveside stood many of Montana's most influential citizens.

How odd it would seem to a stranger to see Mary MacLain standing in Broadway with a basket of cold boiled potatoes on one arm, and under the other a bottle of olives, while watching "Callahan the Bum" try to commit suicide by hanging himself to an awning rope in front of a jewelry store, and yet this last, an actual occurrence, attracted no particular attention in Butte.

Butte in her days has had more interesting characters than any city of her size in the world, for they come to the camp from all points of the compass, and from all conditions and walks in life.

It was a great day in Butte when the first taxi cab made its appearance, and much speculation was rife as to the advisability of trying to run them in such a hilly country. Elliott, an old-time hack driver, was one of the first to make the experiment. One day he came to grief, but there was a very humorous side to it. He was driving his taxi up the hill from the lower depot, and was about a half block from the Great Northern tracks when the warning bell rang and the gates were lowered. The taxi did not slacken its speed, and onlookers heard the driver's voice as the machine smashed through both gates, "Whoa! Whoa, damn you! Whoa!" The car ran into a telegraph pole a few feet beyond, and when Elliott was rescued and unhurt, he smiled apologetically as he said, "I forgot I was not driving the grays." He was still holding fast to the steering wheel, but both feet were through the windshield.

In early days, Senator Clark and Judge Davis were the only men allowed to wear a boiled shirt and starched collar, this privilege being granted them because they both had some money when they came to the camp.

Judge Davis had two suits of clothes, one he bought to wear to Paris when he went to that city to negotiate the sale of the Lexington Mine. Upon his return to America he left the suit in New York, donned the old clothes and again started West. After his death, a relative applied for letters of administration in New York, claiming the deceased left personal property in that state. Upon investigation it was found the personal property consisted of this suit of clothes.

Marcus Daly came to the camp with a pack on his back. F. Augustus Heinze came in later years. He was a polished society gentleman, a college graduate, and a young man of moderate means. They all became multi-millionaires, and all except Senator Clark have passed away. The money accumulated by these four men did more to shape the morale of the people than anything else in the most wonderful state in the Union—wonderful in scenic effect and possibilities, and well deserving the name of Treasure State.

A statue of Daly was placed in the middle of Main Street, just north of the Federal building. One day I listened to two Irishmen as they came down the hill with their dinner buckets, and stopped to inspect the monument. The figure was in dark bronze, and surmounted a granite pedestal. One said to the other, as they gazed at the quiet figure that stood as if looking down over the city, "Och! Mike, I tink it do be a little dark for Daly, it lukes loike a nager, so it do." "Dennis," said the other in an undertone, "sure it is pretty dark, an' O' niver seed Daly carry an overcoat." As they stood talking, a stranger came out of the Post Office and asked one of them to direct him to the Emergency Hospital. "Sure O' will," he answered. "Begorra, it be aisy, an' all yese got to do is to go into Crowley's saloon an' say something agin the Irish an' yese will wake up there, sure yese will."

One afternoon I was passing through the lobby of the Waldorf-Astoria in New York when I heard a voice call "Mistah Davis." I looked around and saw the speaker sitting in what is called "Peacock Alley." It was "Buckets," who a few years past had been a race-track "tout" in Butte. "Ah-s waitin' foah Mistah 'Easy Johnson,' " he said, "an' when Ah saw you, Ah thought Ah would like to speak to you, foah you was always a gentleman, an' always spoke pleasantly to 'Buckets.' "

I asked him how long he had been East. "Ah-s been down in New Jersey a-lookin' after some bosses, an' thought Ah-d like to see New York befoah going back to Butte. Mistah Davis," he said with a happy smile, as he straightened his red and black striped tie, and eased the starched collar, "Ah-s been bustin' in society since you left Butte. Needn't tell you nothing about the game, foah you have played it strong an' knows all the curves. Ah was ast to a dinner at one of yo' friend's house. You know that 'swell' guy what's from here, an' is president of the States Savings? Well, he was one of um, an' Ah understand requested my presence. All went well until the ice cream was served, an' them 'swell' guys commenced to eat it with forks. Ah didn't dare take no chanst of it drippin' through the prongs, so Ah quietly slipped some on mah knife, an' befoah Ah made mah mouth, it slipped off and fell in mah lapt. Guess Ah must ha' been eatin' something hot with the knife. Ah was there with the conversation all right, for they didn't none of them know nuthin' about bosses, an' let me talk. Them 'swell' guys jest set back an' never had nuthin' to say, jest give me the floor an' let me talk, while the ladies showed their appreciation."

It is interesting to watch a black and white shepherd dog at night as he guards two cows that come out of Dublin Gulch to feed on garbage from cans that stand in alleys, or on the edge of sidewalks. Each cow has her different cans, and the dog quietly watches to see that they are not molested. When they have made the rounds they return to the Gulch where they chew their cud and sleep on the granite slopes of the old residential section that was at one time the exclusive home of the Irish—the Finlanders are interlopers, and the section is fast losing caste. It is a narrow place extending into the richest bill in the world, and almost in the center of the city. The little cabins are built close together and close to the road. It is called Anaconda Road, for the famous Anaconda mine is on the hill just above. A passer-by often receives a rotten egg or over-ripe vegetable in the back, but is wise enough not to investigate.

At one time a hanging was to take place in the jail yard. There was a rooming-house close by and the windows of some of the rooms looked out upon the grounds of the yard. The woman conducting the house came to me and said, "I am going to give a little hanging party in the morning and would like to have you join us. It will be quiet, just a congenial few. The view will be better than standing in the yard." I told her I was sorry, but I had a wedding engagement in the morning. A respected and popular old-timer had come to me and said, "I think you are a good friend of mine and that I can trust you. My eldest child is to be married tomorrow, and says the wedding would be a happier one if Papa and Mama would get married first, so I have arranged to be married early before the wedding guests arrive, and want you to be one of the witnesses. The public will never suspect, for they have never known the bride's name, and a license would mean nothing to them."

In early days, before the time of the stage-coach and railroad, caravans would meet on the plains and young people fall in love, and many began housekeeping in a prairie schooner with the honest intention of marrying when they reached a place where there was a minister. Some put it off from time to time; merely a case of honest procrastination.

A lifelong friend of the hero gave the details of the following and a writer wove it into a pretty romance.

One of Butte's prominent citizens is a popular and lovable character who, when Montana was a territory, drove a "bull team," and in later years held one of the highest political offices the State has to bestow upon a citizen. In his younger life he was a saloon-keeper for one night, and the story as it is told is full of pathos and jocose combined. The young man gave up freighting and became operator at a lonely place where the rattle-snake and sage-brush thrive. There were only two buildings in the place—the one where he held forth and another occupied by a woman and her daughter who gave meals to the freighters and whoever chanced to be going that way.

The mother washed clothes for the young operator and many cowboys who came from miles away, and soon a jealous feeling filled the heart of the young man as he saw the "cowpunchers" take long walks with the daughter, and he often said to himself, "It is wonderful how many things a 'cowpuncher' can find that require washing." As time passed the young man's heart became more restless. "I'll fix them," he thought; "she loves music and I used to play the concertina. I'll send to Salt Lake City for one." A few weeks thereafter, when a train of freighters halted at the widow's for the middle-day meal, a square box was carried to the operator's building. He knew the meaning and was restless for night to come when he might unpack the box. "I'll walk way down the trail where they cannot hear me," he mused, "and practise some before she knows I have it."

The evening was beautiful on the prairie, almost a desert sunset as the big ball of fire quietly sank behind the sagebrush. Sunset on the wild range is most wonderful in effect, and the crimson glow that follows would lead the stranger to feel that the heavens were afire. The green, purple shadows of the brush are mystic, and where the glow reaches, the sheen is like waves of fire. This evening, the sunset hour was fascinatingly beautiful, and the widow and daughter came to where he was to enjoy it with him. He wished to get away, and to him the twilight seemed, oh, so long. At last darkness spread over all, and his friends went to their home for the night. When all was quiet he stole out and walked quickly down the lonesome trail that buffalo and other wanderers of the plains had made during their daily pilgrimage to a creek that lay a mile away, a place where they could drink and wallow in the cool waters. He did not know a wandering band of Crees were camping near the creek. The moon was far in the heavens when he left the trail and sat down in a clump of sagebrush, and in the quiet spot began his practise. He had been there about half an hour when he heard a weird, dirge-like chant and the soft beating of tom-toms.

The sounds grew nearer and nearer, until at last four Indians stopped in the trail near where he sat. One came to him and spoke in Cree dialect. He understood, and came out of the brush and tried to explain, but they did not know his meaning and escorted him to their camp, where a fire had been made, and in the glare he saw an Indian maiden standing before a tepee. Like a flash, the meaning dawned upon him. According to Indian tradition, he had proposed to the maiden, and in return had been accepted, and they were about to celebrate the betrothal. A young Indian buck falling in love with a maiden and wishing to make her his squaw, at night stands alone near her tepee and plays on a musical instrument. If his love is reciprocated, the maiden comes forth and silently stands in front of her father's tepee. If rejected, there is no sign of life around the place.

They attributed the distance and hiding in the brush to timidity on the part of the young pale-face. He was lodged in a tepee with the Chief. In the morning, he again tried to explain, but preparations for the celebration went on. Two days had passed when four cowboys rode into the freighting station. The widow and daughter were almost beside themselves with grief and fear, as they told the story of the disappearance. The empty box was there, but no one knew what it had contained.

The cowboys knew an Indian camp was not far away. They examined the ground around the buildings, but wind had blown dust over all signs of footprints. One of the "cowpunchers" wandered along the trail until he came to a sheltered spot, and there found footprints leading in the direction of the camp. He knew the prints were those of a white man, for they were not pigeon-toed as all Indian's are.

He quickly returned to the station and soon four horsemen were off and riding at good speed in the direction in which the Indian camp lay. When they reached the place, the Indians showed a defiant spirit and it was difficult to appease them. The chief argued that it was either a proposal of marriage or an attempt to lure the maiden from her people, but after much talk, both pleasant and threatening, the cowboys rode out of the camp with the young man sitting behind one of the laughing boys. As they left the place they heard a threatening grunt, a guttural sound peculiar to the Indian.

In face of all the pleasantry, the rescued man felt very kindly towards his deliverers, and they were overjoyed to see the musical instrument, and to know he played it, and they made that another excuse to visit the freighting station. "We can take turns dancing with the girl," said one, as they rode away; and soon his one-room building became a rendezvous for "freighters" and "cowpunchers."

"I believe I'll make some money out of these fellows," he mused, as he watched about half a dozen chaparejo-bedecked "cowpunchers" dismount and run the lariat through rings they had fastened in the side of his building, for there were no trees in the neighborhood, "then marry the girl and leave the country. I'll send to Ogden and get a keg of whiskey, and peddle it to them at so much 'per.' "

Each night since his rescue he had played for them to dance, and it robbed him of the hours he might otherwise have spent with the young woman. About a month later, while two cowboys stood in his doorway, two "freighters" lifted from a freight-wagon a large size keg and a small box, and one said, as he placed the box on top of the keg, "Guess that be a faucet for the cider," and with a smile winked at the onlookers. After the train had passed on, "Southern Jack" quizzed the young man as to the meaning of the whiskey being left there, and after much persistence forced an explanation. "It will be a good time to advertise," he thought, as he asked them to help him roll the keg in and tap it. "I'll give them a glass or two and then tell them my intentions."

After he had explained to them and they had taken a few drinks. Jack said with much spirit, "We'll have a reg'ler party the openin' night."

"Have the wimmen bake up everything," said the other, "an' make the date as near pay-day as possible." When details had been arranged and the two "punchers" mounted their horses and started off, "Southern Jack" called back, "We all will be thar," and sure enough, during the afternoon of the opening day in all directions over the range could be seen little coils of dust rising from trails. It was made by the hoofs of horses hurrying along carrying guests to the dance. Those who had reached there early had arranged a stage for the orchestra and bar, by placing two dry-goods boxes close together, and when the hour came for the festivities to begin, the young man with the concertina on his lap sat on one box and the keg of whiskey on the other. Mother and daughter both joined in the dancing, and all went well for several hours.

Between dances the guests would help themselves to liquid refreshments and then drop a silver piece in a tin cup that stood close by. About three o'clock in the morning, trouble began, and the jingling of spurs that kept time with the concertina became louder and faster and then a few shots were fired through the ceiling; then a jealous fight over the daughter, then the mother, and then more drinks, and some became drowsy, while others seemed to take pleasure in shooting through walls and ceiling. The mother and daughter escaped and went to their building. The young man, with trembling hands and feet, played on, but the music was fast and disconnected.

At last quiet came, and at the break-o'-day he silently rolled the keg to the door and turned on the faucet, and what was left of the whiskey flowed to the ground below. As he went back to his room his eyes rested on sleeping "cowpunchers" in the corners and all about the floor. It was his first and last night as a bartender.

The first mail leaving the place carried his resignation, and he journeyed on to Butte, where he still lives and enjoys the friend^ of frontier days.

One of Butte's mining men, a prominent and picturesque character around the city, confided in me and told me the secret of his good health and how he guarded against pneumonia. "From the time of the first frost in the fall," he said, "I never bathe until after the last frost of Spring. The oil," he said, "from the body forms a coating and is like an extra skin and helps to keep out the chill." While listening to him I said to myself, "What a joy this story would be to the small boy." The first frost usually is in September, and the last in June. It would give the small boy ten months of happiness.

A young woman who had experienced many of the trials of life married one of Butte's wealthiest young men, and began housekeeping in what is thought to be the finest residence in the city. She was happy—oh, so happy, and proud of her home. Among the wedding presents was a splendid copy of a Rembrandt. Visitors would come to pay a call and most all gave expression of their admiration of the picture. "What a beautiful Rembrandt," some would say, or, "Isn't that splendid." And the young matron would reply in her pleasing manner, "Yes, it is pretty," or, "I love it." It seemed to get on her nerves, but she did not say anything about it until one day an intimate girl friend, whose nickname was "Mike," called on her, and in her effervescent manner exclaimed, "Oh! What a stunning Rembrandt!" The young matron stepped back, and placing a hand on each hip, said, "Mike, who in hell is Rembrandt?"

A few years ago two prominent men, both prominent politicians, got mixed up in an amusing social affair that afterwards led them into the divorce court. They were an

Irishman and a Jew. Just for convenience we will call the Jew "Mose" and the Irishman, "Dan." They were both named as co-respondents and many people felt that the Irishman was guilty and the Jew innocent, but in his nervousness he convicted himself. It was a case of two married women of another city and one of the husbands was the plaintiff.

It was Dan who introduced Mose to the women. He was bright, but unscrupulous, and planned to use the Jew; and on the other hand the Jew was loyal and in trying to protect the Irishman, surrounded himself with circumstantial evidence which convicted him, and in his honesty convicted Dan. He was unaccustomed to court proceedings and did not understand, and how often that is the case where a witness is honest and wishes to explain.

I was in court and witnessed the proceedings. They were both called by the plaintiff. Dan had been on the stand and the attorneys for the plaintiff got very little from him that was material. Mose was nervous and turned deathly pale as the attorney for the plaintiff said, "Will Mr. Dinklvich please take the stand?"

The witness did not leave his seat, and the attorney spoke to him again: "Will the witness please take the stand?"

He looked frightened as he answered, "I can't do it, I can't stand up."

A wave of amusement passed over the room as the Judge said, "Will the bailiff please assist the witness to the chair?"

He was tired and excitable after the long direct examination. Up to this time he had been a poor witness for the plaintiff, for his cross-examination will show how he had been approached by the attorney for the wife, a procedure undignified but not uncommon. The attorney for the defendant began, as he watched the man closely, "Mr. Dinklvich—" but he got no further. The witness became very much excited; he raised his right hand out towards the attorney and the left towards the Judge and began to speak in an almost incoherent manner. "Dan Kavin got me into dese troubles," he said, "an' I got ze voist of it."

There was much sympathy for the fellow, for there had been much sparring between the attorneys and he was confused as well as very tired.

"The witness will please answer the questions, 'yes' or 'no,' and refrain from comment," said the attorney.

"I know vot to say, Mr. Skviggs," he continued; "you tole me vot to say an' I can say it if you do not got me rattled. I haf been in ze court-room efery day since ze case began an' I haf noticed ze vitnesses got rattled—"

"Please just answer my questions—yes or no," said the lawyer.

"I know vot to say, Mr. Skviggs; but if ze Judge overrule an' sustain me I vill got rattled an' lie like Dan Kavin did."

The court-room rang loud with sounds of the gavel as the onlookers became boisterous. Mr. Squig looked around in despair while the witness insisted upon talking. The Judge again admonished the onlookers.

"If quiet is not maintained," he said, "I shall ask the bailiff to clear the court-room and the proceedings will be continued behind closed doors. I would suggest that as the witness is unduly nervous he be let to proceed in his own way and tell of his doings at the Van Lennop home."

"That is vot I vont to do," said the excited man, turning to the Judge, "an' I vont to remember vot Mr. Skviggs tole me vot to say, but if I am overruled and sustained I vill forgot."

As he spoke, he nervously glanced to where the plaintiff sat, for the practical joker had told him Mr. Van Lennop was armed and would shoot at the least provocation.

"Ven Dan Kavin and me go up to ze Van Lennop house," he continued, "Dan he say to me before ve start, 'Now, Mose, ven ve got up to ze house Maggie is your goil,' an' ven I see her I knows I got ze voist of it. Ven de music vos started in ze parlor Maggie she say to me, 'Mr. Dinklvich, ve take a valk in ze garden,' an' ven ve got dare she say, 'Mr. Dinklvich, ve sit here in ze bright moonlight.' Ven ve comes back an' Dan Kavin vos singing 'Silver Threads mit derr Golt.' An' ven he got through Mrs. Van Lennops she took him too mit ze garden. Ven ve vere alone Maggie she got ze family albums."

The attorney vigorously protested, "I wish to excuse the witness," he said in a voice trembling with disgust. "This sort of business is all out of order." The Judge paid no attention to him but turned to the witness and quietly said, "The witness may proceed."

"I forgot me vot I vos saying."

"You were just starting to tell us about the family album," said the Judge.

"Oh, yes; vell, Maggie she got ze family albums an' she opens it an' she say, 'Mr. Dinklvich, zis eis little Timmy, my youngist brudder, an' zis eis Jackie.' An' you aut haf seen it. An' zen she say, 'Zis is me ven I vus sixteen.' An' I say, 'It haf keep vel.' An' she shut ze album an' lay it on ze table an' move her chair close to me an' take me mine hand in hers an' look up mit mine eyes an' say, 'Mose,' an' I look at her an' I vanted to, oh, how I vanted to, but I couldn't do it, I shut me mine eyes an' say to me, 'Mose, be a good sport.' "

There was a hush in the court-room. The audience leaned forward in their seats, full of expectancy.

"Ven I opens me mine eye. she vos just ze same. I say, 'Maggie, rest back in ze chair,' an' she did, an' I put me a pillow under her head an' close me mine eyes an' sing so fine as I could a Yiddish love song, an' ven I finish me mine song I opens mine eyes an' Maggie vos sound asleep. She fall asleep ven she hear mine soft notes full off tears—"

"Your honor, I again ask to excuse the witness," said the attorney appealingly. The Judge gave the attorney a look of disgust as he said, "The witness may continue his story."

"Mine foder send me oud to see more of ze voild an' I see too much. Ve all got drunk an' vere up all night an' I vos hungry an'—"

"I think," said the Judge, "we can see to what extent the witness was coached. I will excuse him."

"Just one moment," suggested the plaintiff's attorney, "I wish to ask the witness one question. Mr, Dinklvich, are you telling the truth, the whole truth, and nothing but the truth?"

"Yes," he honestly answered.

"You know the seriousness of the oath, do you not?"

"Yes; I know vot it means an' I am honest. Ze greatest compliment a person can gif me is to say I am a vite Jew."

"That is all," said the attorney with much satisfaction. It is not necessary to tell how the case was decided.

I have seen attorneys go so far in arguing a case to the jury as to hold a twenty-dollar gold piece in the palm of their hand. It meant this and more to follow.

In early days, during exceedingly trying times, a deacon of the Mountain View Methodist Church was sheriff.

I knew a society woman who, when going out and anxious to get a message to her husband as soon as he returned home, would tie a note to the neck of the whiskey bottle before leaving the house.

A society matron who was very fond of the races and who never missed an opportunity to attend always held a rosary in her hand while placing a bet or talking with a "tout."

Chapter Eleven

AT THE OLD COUNTRY CLUB

The porch of the Country Club that stood on the "Flat" near the four cemeteries, a slaughter-house and brick-yard, was brilliantly lighted with Chinese lanterns. Here and there a "cozy nook" protected by fresh green pines brought from the mountains, gave seclusion to "timid sparks."

A warm grate fire, in a measure, relieved the cold, cheerless effect of the dance hall. The unplaned rafters, high ceilings and weather-board sides, made the place a barren, unattractive looking room. In a bay window, an orchestra was stationed. The handsome, but over-decorated table placed in this wooden Sahara was like an oasis in a desert. Its wonderful pile of bloom lacked refinement and the artistic touch of culture. The host had purposely over-embellished, for he wished to dazzle some whom he had invited, and in that way study their mental strength and see in what capacity they might be used. The waiters had been instructed to keep the glasses well filled, and had carefully followed instructions.

Our host met us at the door as we entered. Formality had been laid aside for this night, as many of those bidden would not understand. The dinner guests had arrived and were soon seated at the table, and when the time came for the dance guests to arrive, all at the table were in a jovial spirit.

A carriage drove up to the entrance and soon two men entered the hall, one a stranger from Boston. As the door closed behind them, a young doctor who had imbibed too freely, rose from his chair and soon a ripe tomato, with a little dressing on the side, landed on the Bostonian's right eye. He gracefully acknowledged the unusual salutation and passed on to a room where men removed their wraps.

This seemed a signal for a "rough house." The dinner guests left the table and gathered in small groups here and there where they might have a liquor and cigarette and be undisturbed by the noisy throng that began to invade the hall.

Some retired to the outer balcony, for the moonlit night was balmy for an autumn night in the mountains.

In the room where the Bostonian went to leave his top coat and hat was an improvised bar. Three of the men who had been dinner guests were stationed at this place, while three others formed themselves into a committee to escort every newcomer to the bar, and when there he was compelled to drink five cocktails. When an obstreperous guest was encountered, a member of the committee would state to him, "It's to even up the party. We have been at it for two hours. Come—be a sport and take your medicine like a man."

They knew the consequence of a refusal. The scheme had the desired effect, and soon the hall was filled with merry dancers, and the music changed from the classic strains of the seductive waltz and two-step to a gay "rag-time."

"I can feel the vibration of the building," my companion laughed heartily.

"Yes; it is like a swaying mob, isn't it?" I answered, and then suggested we go to the gallery where we might sit and look on. We climbed the rickety steps that led to the balcony and took seats near a suspiciously frail-looking rail.

The butcher, the baker and the candlestick maker were all there on the floor, below. They were lined up for inspection, and in most cases there was not an exchange of mentality, or harmony of souls. There were some strong characters lined up, but treacherous, for they would not stay bought.

"How interesting to look on," she said, as she moved close to the rail.

"Such manner of entertaining is not very elevating," I said, "but is common here. It's just a little flattery for the poor 'boobs,' and they fall for it, and in that fall will go the limit."

"It does seem strange that in this day and age a person has a price for his manhood," was her only answer as she quietly looked on.

"And some sell mighty cheap and seem to like being 'crooks.' It sort of gives them standing to be associated with the wealthy criminals."

I leaned back in my chair and watched her interested expression as she watched the throng of dancers.

A BUCKING PINTO

"I have always wanted to look on at a cowboy dance," she said, without taking her eyes from the floor below. "Have you ever attended one?"

"Yes," I said; "I remember a rather lively one up in the Big Hole country."

"Tell me about it. It must have been interesting." She was all attention as she moved back and closer to me. "Do they really shoot up everything?" I merely smiled as I launched into the story.

"A 'tenderfoot' friend of mine who had been in the camp for several weeks wanted to go for a long horseback journey. I planned a trip for him up through the Big Hole to the old battlefield and back through the Wise river country. We went by train to the Divide and there took saddle horses. I had wired for horses, and when we reached our rail destination and went to the stable we found two horses already saddled and waiting: one a handsome large sorrel, the other a little dark brown 'cayuse.' "

"Tell me," she interrupted, "what is the definition of 'cayuse'?"

"Just a name for an Indian pony," I answered.

"I wondered. I have heard so many Butte people called that."

"That's because they are wild and unbroke," I smiled, as I continued the story. "My friend, for the first time, showed selfishness by stepping forward and starting to mount the fine-looking animal. I stood and watched him ride out of the corral, and then turned to where stood my little horse, blear-eyed and sleepy-looking, with head hanging down towards his knees. I knew the specimen and was satisfied. The big range saddle almost covered his back.

"We started out, crossed the river and followed the left bank. My little horse, all skin and bones, moved on with gait like the rocking of a cradle, picking his way over rocks and rough roads. Far in the distance we could see the glistening snowcaps of the Goat Mountains that rise above one of the Indian battlefields of early days.

"We had gone but a few miles when I noticed my friend now and then slide over to one side of the saddle, while his fine-looking horse came down with a heavy thud.

"Our first stop was at Dewey's Flats, a little town with one street, lined on either side by log cabins; a truly frontier town. No sidewalks; everybody walked in the middle of the road.

"We reached the little tavern just before the noon hour. In the dining-room a pretty half-breed girl waited on the table. Her straight, black hair hung in two strands over her shoulders in truly Indian fashion, for they were in front and fell about to her knees. She was a handsome girl to look at. Her soft, brown-red complexion and large, dreamy black eyes made a wonderful picture.

"I paid no attention to her, merely giving my order. My friend at once started to 'josh' her and that is where he lost out, for the Indian has much dignity.

"There was to be a show in town that night, so we stayed over. For about a week or ten days, word had been passed through the country telling of the event to come. Chairs and tables in a saloon and gambling house had been removed so as to give room for the performance and dance that was to follow. The show people carried with them an orchestra consisting of one violinist—and that was the incentive for the dance.

"About three o'clock that afternoon I sat down to an old foot-pedal organ that stood in a corner of a little sitting-room.

"Soon the young waitress came from the kitchen and, without speaking, moved a chair close to the end of the organ and sat quietly listening to me play Moody and Sankey hymns, for that was the extent of music they possessed. My friend again tried to flirt with her.

" 'You're going to the dance with me tonight, aren't you?' he said in a flippant manner.

"She did not look towards him, but with a guttural sound, characteristic to the Indian before speaking, said, 'No, I go with him,' pointing her hand towards me. I was game; stopped pumping the old machine, turned to her and said, 'Yes, and we'll go to the show first, won't we?'

"Not a smile passed her lips as she answered, 'Yes, we go to the show.'

"I took her to the show and we all stayed for the dance. Chaparejo bedecked 'cowpunchers,' with high-heel boots and rattling spurs, were there. Prospectors and ranchers with their wives and sweethearts came from miles around to attend the affair. My girl danced with all the rhythm of the Indian, spoiling it now and then by a long drawn out pivot, merely to show the pale face she understood their ways.

"All went well until about midnight and then trouble seemed to be in the air, for her sweetheart—a 'cowpuncher' from up near Wisdom—arrived upon the scene and at once became mean. As whiskey became more plentiful, threats of bodily injury were often made to me as he took more drinks.

"I knew enough not to try and explain matters, for in that state there was no reasoning.

"As the jealous lover became well intoxicated, he leaned against the bar, one foot resting on the brass railing, and in a loud voice began to upbraid the girl, emphasizing his remarks now and then by a shot through the ceiling or floor. He ground his teeth as he became more unsteady and wild-eyed with anger.

"Seemingly paying no attention to him, I invited all to have a drink. There was a rush to the bar. The excited lover turned and faced a whiskey bottle, and while he was pouring out a generous drink I quietly passed around to where he stood and in a rather flippant manner said, 'Pard, why don't you sometime come over to Butte and make us a visit?' It had the desired effect, for he poured another drink.

"There is always a chance of a bad shooting when a fellow drinks too much."

"Tell me about the rest of the trip," she said, in much interest. "It is all new to me."

"There was nothing of particular interest until the day and night before we returned to Dewey on our way back to Butte. I wanted to show my friend the Vipond country. We turned up the road leading along Wise river. At dusk we left the road to follow a trail that led through a stretch of timber. Night had just closed in when we reached a spot where there had been a forest fire; burned trees had fallen and obliterated the trail, and soon I realized we were lost. The moon came up and we kept on going, now and then the horses stepping over a fallen tree. In the moonlight each stump looked like an Indian or bear, but we drove ahead, now and then reining in when one of the horses would snort as if scenting danger.

"Just after the break-o'-day we ran across a dreadfully unkempt-looking man lying fast asleep beside a large log. When we roused him I recognized the man known throughout that section as the 'Wild Man.' Wherever night overtook him he lay down to sleep. Prospectors and hunters would give him ammunition, and when he shot a deer or elk, he would camp there until he had devoured it all. A place he called home was in the woods near a small cave. A few poles leaning up against a tree constituted his summer home, and the cave was where he spent much time in the winter. His long, unkempt hair was in thirteen strands, braided as it grew longer, and most everything under the sun braided in it, giving him a mighty wild appearance.

"He directed us to the trail leading to Vipond Park. We found we had been wandering around during the long night in a radius of about a mile.

"At one place on the trail we looked through a hiatus in the mountains and in the distance of about seventy miles saw Butte on the barren mountain side. The atmosphere was so clear we could almost distinguish the different mines.

"It was a pretty ride from Vipond back to Dewey's. As we turned in on the one road leading through town, we passed a wagon just leaving. On the high seat of the dead-ax wagon I recognized my little half-breed and her sweetheart. As we passed they both looked straight ahead, with no sign of recognition. When we reached the little hotel, the landlady told us the fellow refused to leave until the girl married him."

"Watch them now," the listener interrupted.

The music had stopped. Some of the dancers flocked to the punch-bowl; others to the small room where stronger drinks were served. Women, with glass of wine or highball in one hand and cigarette in the other, walked with their partners to the outer gallery. Some found seats in cozy nooks; others stood blowing loud applause through the hall.

My companion was much interested as I pointed out the professional reformers, limelight seekers and those of other professions.

"This all sounds and looks more like the Butte I have read about."

"We have some wonderfully fine lonesome people in Butte," I suggested. "Lonesome because they will not mingle. They have not had an opportunity to meet the right ones. They are invited to an affair like this. They look on and then decide to retire to a quiet life during their sojourn in the camp."

"You do not paint your aristocracy in very glowing colors," she said, with a twinkle in the eye.

"It is a queer conception of life most of them have. There are three periods of aristocracy," I answered, not taking my eyes from the floor below. "They are birth, wealth and worth. We have long since passed through the first, and are now on our way through the second, and I am glad to say, almost at the end. How splendid it will be when we enter the third—the aristocracy of worth. When people will be received for what they are and what they have done. The leaven is working fast and a new spirit is rising."

Dawn's silver light was putting the stars to flight as we left the barren club house. Some were still dancing, others lounging in "cozy nooks," some taking carriages for road-houses that dot the "Flat," where they might have more dancing, more drinks and a breakfast before returning home, while many, like ourselves, drove out of the grounds and along a road that led up the mountain side to the city.

"Jack seems to be in a hurry," said the young lady as the lash fell on one of the horses.

"Yes," I laughed, "but he will be too late for a game of poker. He is a great gambler and often stakes his all. One night he sat in a game and luck was against him until the last round of 'Jack-pots.' He was 'strapped' when he filled his hand. His watch and finger-ring were in the pot. He had drawn a good hand but had nothing left to bet. At last he said as he took out his false-teeth, 'How much be these worth?' It was at a time when dentistry was crude and gold plates were made heavy. The plate was appraised and placed in the pot and he win.

"Why do you say 'win'?" she asked.

"It's just a sporting term," I answered. "Won might cause much confusion in enumerating at a horse race and such as that."

Chapter Twelve

CORRUPTING FELLOW MEN

The world over when one mentions Butte, people ask why Butte has such an unenviable reputation. Fear and hypocrisy are the prime reasons. The gardens of life are unkept by those who ought to be guardians and the weeds of corruption smother and warp young life. A scientist at one time said he believed the peculiar mental condition of so many in Butte was due in a way to the barrenness of the place and radioactive minerals. He said a person living in direct contact of rays from the mineral would soon feel the effect. The brain becomes metallic and they are not wholly responsible.

The voyage of life to many in Butte is tumultuous. In an old gallery in a foreign land there hangs a set of pictures that depict the voyage of life. The first canvas shows the background, laid in, in the impressionist. Some might imagine it to be a cliff; others the mouth of a large cave. Floating on the waters of a placid stream that comes from this darkness is a bark filled with beautiful flowers. Lying in the center of the mass of bloom is a young babe. On the prow, with celestial light about her, stands an angel with trumpet in one hand, heralding to the world the birth of the child; in the other hand she holds an hour-glass, the upper globe filled with sands of time.

The second canvas shows everything bright and cheerful. The waters of the stream glisten in the sunshine. On the banks of the stream of mirror-clear waters are many young trees, palms and brilliant blossoms. In the bright sky above, resting on silvery clouds, is a wonderful castle. In the prow of the barge stands a youth, his eyes turned towards the castle as if riveted there. The angel has left the bark and stands on the shore waving a Godspeed to the boy who is just going out into the world. The hour-glass rests on the prow of the boat.

The third canvas shows a man standing in the center of the boat. There are many rocks in the stream and the troubled waters are filled with corruption; broken branches lie here and there among withered palms. The barge rocks and plunges as it moves on towards the distant rapids, and there he stands gazing on the half-empty hour-glass.

The fourth canvas shows an old man standing in the bark with his arms reaching out as if to receive some one. All about is darkness; the celestial light shines on his upturned brow. In the heavens the clouds are billowy and bright. Many angels float through space beckoning the old man home. The upper globe of the hour-glass is empty. He had finished this life and was steering his boat ashore. He had passed through corruption and gone over the rapids, and again his eyes turn to the celestial light.

Managers of Butte combines feel safe behind the subservient press. They use much gold in the miscarriage of justice and corrupting their fellow man. Pressure is brought to bear on weak people and they fall, and in that fall seem to lose all sense of honor. They go the limit.

Some place one foot in state prison, while others stand with the noose dangling just above their heads. The real criminal sits in his office, club or home while his agents deal out the corrupting stuff, and hire character assassins to ruin the standing of people who oppose him.

Some sell themselves to high bidders merely to be used as dummies, or like the decoy duck. For the price they have sold their soul, they stand ready to be set up and knocked down at any time, or accept anything the occasion demands.

They remind me of a ram with a bell tied around his neck. A ram that was kept in a sheep corral of a slaughter-house at the stockyards in Chicago. He was there to lead his unsuspecting friends to their death. He would circulate around amongst the hungry and frightened sheep and when a sufficient number were following him he would quietly walk up an incline run that led to a closed door of the slaughter-house. When his followers crowded around him the door would be thrown open and he would walk in and his friends follow. When the death room was filled with his wondering friends, the door would be closed behind, shutting off retreat. He would then walk to another closed door, where stood a man ready to open it for him. It opened to another incline that led to the same corral where he repeated his act of deception.

Women have been brought into the camp for the purpose of corrupting judges and have succeeded, and after being used, tossed aside like an old rag. In early days I have seen men lined up in a row receiving money for their votes, selling their manhood for a few dollars. I have known women in Butte ready to sell themselves to the highest bidder; women who belong to what is known as the fashionable set.

Some of Butte's leaders argue that indiscretions may be overlooked in that set. If that be a conventionality of that set how preferable the other set is, those who may not be so influential; to whom fortune and trickery have not given so much of this world's goods; where the milk of human kindness runs through the veins; where hypocrisy is little known. There are no two rules with reference to propriety in the conduct of true man or womanhood. People never attain a position in which they can violate the things that go for decency, ignore them and excuse it because of self, because they may have attained what they think is a more exalted social position.

There are no two standards of morality: one for Butte and one for some other place. There are men in Butte who are moral curses to the world. Men who wink at the robbery of people's money and at the robbery of little children. Men who haven't the well-opened eyelid or untiring gaze of the honest man. In speaking with them, there is no stamp of candor in the voice. They drop the eye to hide the duplicity. They sit back like cowards and have others do the criminal work, sowing seeds in youth that are in maturity harvested, and what is the crop? Criminals—is the only answer.

Do the people decry this state of affairs? No! Most of them applaud and say they are good business men, and the professional howler stands around the streets howling for them: men who are paid handsomely for telling of the wealthy criminal's beautiful traits of character and his many charitable acts the public are not cognizant of. Men who owe their wealth to some person's ruin never see the sunny side of life; their nights are cold and cheerless. Their slogan is: "If you haven't anything authentic, frame up something." They never experience the great needs of the heart; the sympathy, the vibrating harmony of souls, and without a generous thought or close fellowship their lives dry and crumble like the leaves of a fading year. One night during recent labor troubles, I went down on the "Flat" where I could look back and see the searchlights in action. It was beautifully weird, and to one who realized the conditions as they exist in Butte, a fascinating tragedy. Night shut from view the ugliness and barrenness of the city on the hill, and all one could see was the fantastic electrical display—a sight for the romanticist. Searchlights were in every direction. A brilliant glare, like the tail of a meteor or shooting-star, shone from what seemed to be the eyes of a dragon. One from the brow of the mountain would slowly move around like the winged serpent turning its head, crossing perhaps one in the valley or on a hill or dump. Sometimes the incandescent rays would meet and remain stationary. Then I saw flashes from what seemed to be immovable lights, like the blaze of Dante's column. They were signal lights sending their message of hatred and class war. It was a sad, beautiful tragedy, for one class of human beings was searching for those of another class.

Chapter Thirteen

THE CRIME OF BLACKMAIL

In a mining camp where hundreds have staked their all on a chance for quick wealth, where life itself is regarded as a gamble and held cheaply; where the end always justifies the means, and the means are far too often worse than questionable, as a natural sequence, following closely on the heels of the more open corruptionist we find the jackal of crime, the blackmailer.

In Butte, the victims of blackmail are numbered in the hundreds, and the proudest, the mightiest and best have paid their unwilling tribute.

Blackmail is not only a heinous offense, but a very common one, few cases ever coming into public notice. In very many instances it is successful, the circumstances being such as to convince the victim that "division and silence" is better than the train of evils that might otherwise follow. Quite often the crime is so shrewdly planned as to evade detection, in which case it seldom finds its way to publicity, whether the victim is or is not disposed to settle the matter with the criminal. In the nature of the offense, blackmail is one of the most despicable crimes in the roster of criminal possibilities, for while it partakes of the nature of robbery, not only of money and property, but character, it may be infinitely worse when the threat is carried into effect. Murder, arson, and a dozen other crimes may be woven into the possible results of blackmail.

A man may hold an important position where he learns many secrets of the corporation employing him. He has a misunderstanding with some official— a meeting is held and he is voted out. He may get into some serious trouble. He may commit murder, arson, or sedition. All he has to do is to say to his former employers, "You protect me in my crimes or I will expose you in yours," and he is protected while the flame of hatred burns in their breasts.

Another fellow persuades some weak character to commit perjury for him. He is asked to do it again, but demurs. Threats of prosecution for perjury are made and he says, "I will commit perjury for you, but you must come through with some money, or else I will see that you are prosecuted for instigating perjury," and he comes through. One is the victim of the other, and they must smile and grasp each other by the hand while in public, for the world must not know they all are criminals.

They are starving mental paupers. Their lives are cramped and withered for food of an honest thought. A man's true reward in life is found in his own soul. Some never wear the honest halo of good deeds, or are embalmed by love or garlanded by affections of fellow man, and lonesome they travel through life, and at last night time comes on and there is no sound from the dying lips save the moan of blackened manhood, and when his body is lowered into the grave, people turn away with mingled thoughts.

The fact of Butte's being so thoroughly advertised throughout the world as an extravagantly wealthy place, where people are lavish in expenditure, brings adventurers of all descriptions. Business sharks come with the adventuress, and others come solely for the purpose of blackmail.

At one time, a middle-aged woman, with two young women she called her daughters, came to the city and rented a furnished house. The young women were good-looking and vivacious, and soon met many of the men about town. Not long thereafter, whisperings of peculiar doings were heard, and it was said a prominent politician had been held up for eight hundred dollars. One evening, I met a prominent doctor, and he told me of his experience with the alleged mother, and how he had settled with her by giving her a block of spurious mining stock.

That same evening the alleged mother went to a hotel where a young man lived, called for a "bell hop" and sent her card to the young man. The boy found the intended victim in the lobby. "There is a lady in the parlor wishes to see you," he said, as he handed him the card. The young man went to the room where she was waiting, and she began without formality, "You have been out with my youngest daughter." The young man did not reply, but stood quietly listening. "She has not finished her education, and I want two thousand dollars to send her to a finishing school." The young man then spoke in a quiet, deliberate manner, "I know your game. You have bumped up against the wrong man, and if you and your alleged daughters are not out of Butte inside of twenty-four hours, I will have you jailed for attempting blackmail." A few hours later a train carried them out of the city.

Three months later, the two girls returned to Butte and were inmates of a brothel in the restricted district. The alleged mother has not been heard from.

I will mention just one other case, as it is a splendid illustration as to what extent people will go in crime, and shows how some who are looked upon as respectable will indulge in the "get rich quick" proposition. It is the case of two young men who were supposed to have plenty of money. It was an attempt to extort a large sum of money from these young fellows. It had been planned with much forethought, and some people think that the principal criminals were not apprehended, and their scheme was not carried out, and that was to drive one of the young fellows from the city. In other words, make it so unpleasant for him he would not stay in Butte. He interfered with the high hand of a certain element.

The young men both lived at the same hotel. A young woman came to the city and procured a position as manicurist in the barber shop of the hotel. From there she went to a house of ill repute not far from the hotel.

Now the principals in the case were these: The two young men on the one side, and on the other the ex-manicurist, a doctor, a lawyer whom people in addressing say, the Honorable, a sanctimonious church member, another lawyer who had filled one of the highest state offices the people have to offer to a citizen, and a woman who, it was afterwards learned, was the mistress of the ex-State official.

Threats of a lawsuit were made if the men did not come through with a large amount of money. The threateners were wisely encouraged along to a position where it was either bring the suit or be prosecuted for attempt at blackmail.

The mother of one of the young men lived in an Eastern city. He explained matters to her and she stood firmly by his side. The young fellows, in facing a nasty "frame-up," argued that people who did not stand by them at such a time were not worthy of the name friend. Matters were forced and at last the suit was brought. Several overtures for settlement were made by the plaintiffs. At one stage of the proceedings, the sanctimonious lawyer sent for one of the defendants to come to his office, and when the young man went there, the fellow said, "For two hundred and fifty dollars I will have your name stricken from the proceedings." At the same time, the doctor in the case made the same proposition to the other young fellow.

It was a clever mode of procedure, but it fell through, and a day for the hearing was set. The day before the hearing, the ex-State official called at the office of one of the defendant's attorneys and made a plea to withdraw the case. "I will withdraw the case for two dollars and a half, just what it cost to draw up the complaint." His offer was refused. It was another clever ruse, but did not work.

At ten o'clock in the morning of the day set for the hearing, the plaintiffs were not in Court, neither was the doctor nor sanctimonious lawyer. The ex-State official was there. When the Court convened he had disappeared, and the Judge let the case go over until one o'clock in the afternoon. When that hour came, even the ex-official was not there. This was Monday, and the Judge let it go over until the following Thursday, and when that day came none of the parties to the complaint were to be found, and later on it was learned that the ex-manicurist was an inmate of a brothel in San Francisco, and the other "lady" in the case was a resident of "The Castle," the most exclusive resort in the restricted district of Helena.

Chapter Fourteen

PATRIOTS AND TRAITORS

When the world war began, it seemed in Butte a signal for an orgy of profiteering. Professional flag wavers and other traitors of the rankest type were much in evidence. They were at the head of patriotic parades, and the loudest spouters of "hot air" at meetings. And when lined up against the bar of their club would tell most startling stories of bravery and what they would do if younger—playing to the gallery; a mental condition almost unbelievable. They would give their money, but scheme in some way to get it back from the less fortunate; just a little touch of profiteering here and there.

Some gave wholly for the glory of self-advertising, and humanity was laid aside by the fake philanthropist and limelight seekers.

Many in life's young morning, so mysterious, so splendid, proudly volunteered to go where the war cry of freedom would be loudest and clear, and glory and work came to them blended.

Twilight came and all nature seemed a land of
     dreams
As the sound of music wheeled into the air,
Full of life like the world in springtime teems.
The boys answered the bugle blare.

And then along the quiet street,
Beneath a purple and crimson low-hanging cloud.
Came the muffled sound of many feet
And a wave of colors proud.

They were answering the voice of their Nation.
"Your path of honor is made plain and clear;
Let the gun be a joy—not a yoke;
Let the Star-Spangled Banner fill the air."

They marched by in manly rows ;
Each eye told of the spirit of pride within.
Their cheeks not ashen, but like a rose
In twilight shadows, cool and dim.

Evening glow came stealing through a cloud that
     was fading away.
Like a river ceasing to flow;
Friends waved, "God speed you on your way!"
As they tramped ahead to meet the foe.

It was a glowing crimson time of change,
An evening not to be forgot;
Life throbbing and quivering strong and strange,
As they marched by with never a stop.

The music, not muffled, but soft, gave thrills
To the fathomless dreaming air.
Full of glory and pride, though still.
As they passed their friends standing there.

The air was full of pride and farewell
As they marched along with steady tramp ;
The music was mystic, as soft notes fell
And died in the distance with that tramp, tramp,
    tramp.

Some did not return, for they fell asleep in the glare and
blast of the cannon's roar. In poppy fields of France,
crosses mark the spot where they rest. They were—

Boys whose heart-strings to rest were stilled
Not on the path of Gethsemane;
For their anthem was sung on the battlefield with
    patriotic thrill
Of love and honor by their comrades many.

Boys who would say, "Come away from that path.
That road that leads to Gethsemane;
For we want much cheer right up to the last,
To encourage the weak hearts of many."

Boys who would say, "We have entered the portals
    that lie ahead.
Not the land of Gethsemane;
A land where we speak no such word as dead,
A realm of reward to soldiers many."

From the portals beyond we hear their refrain—
"Let us lead you from the path of Gethsemane;
Our spirits will hover near and mark your path until
    we meet again
Where you will learn the mysteries of life and
    understand—with comrades many."

Those who returned in the noble grace of manhood robed,
and souls throbbing with life and the true feeling of man,
proud and under the flag their fathers flew, with heads

erect, marched through the multitude's roar for the Boys
and the Red, White and Blue.

> Woodlands echoed a new-born day
> Of life full of hope and gleam;
> Now proudly they go their different way,
> Happy to think they helped work out God's scheme.
>
> As peace thrills the tranquil deep,
> And murmuring rhythmic calm fills
> Shadowy vales and prairies that sweep
> Far out towards majestic mountains and rolling
>   hills—

The slacker comes back to town. The draft-evader does
not know the meaning of the word shame any more than
does the profiteer. If he has a slight feeling of a world
glorified by truth and honor, how he must cringe before
memories, for he has no noble recollections of the part he
played.

Chapter Fifteen

THE HANGING OF FRANK LITTLE

A far cry from the rude justice of Vigilante days, the darkest shadow ever placed on Butte's shady canvas was the assassination of Frank Little. Many newswriters tried to dignify the act by the word "lynching." It was not a lynching. It had not the semblance of an early day lynching, when honorable men gave the suspect a fair trial and if he was convicted they hanged him in the presence of the populace.

They were a few masked cowards who went in the dead of night to the victim they knew had been drugged by a traitor and lay sleeping while waiting their coming; his clothes lying over the back of a chair while he quietly slept on. He was an agitator, but had the right to a trial, which was denied him.

In this day and age there are Courts of Justice where people may carry grievances and have them adjusted; but no, they went like animals crazed for blood. They broke down one door but did not find him. They broke down another just across the hall and there found him (as the evidence given at the inquest showed) lying fast asleep. They laid the bedding over the foot of the bed (as the evidence showed) and then dragged the cripple down the stairs and out into the night and then into an automobile that stood in waiting; and quickly drove to a trestle on the outskirts of the city. They were looking for blood and found it, for it came from wounds they inflicted upon the body of their victim before they hanged him to the trestle. This was during recent labor troubles and caused world-wide comment.

The funeral procession of Frank Little formed near the Federal building and the Marcus Daly monument, and it seemed as if Daly stood there upon the granite pedestal a silent looker-on. It was the most unusual funeral procession that has ever passed along the streets of a city. The body reposing in a gray casket over which had been laid a blanket of red bloom, fastened by streamers of ribbon of the same color, was borne on the shoulders of six stalwart men as it was removed from the undertaker's parlor to the street, and there the procession formed and started on the silent march of three miles down the mountain side to a cemetery in the valley.

On the side streets adjacent to Main were societies waiting to fall in line when their turn came. First a band softly playing a funeral dirge moved down the street; then one or two societies, and following on the shoulders of six friends came the casket containing the body. The moving-picture man was there and along the line of march cameras were in windows. Silent men marched four abreast. Women with babes at the breast were in line. Mothers pushed go-carts while fathers carried children who were not able to walk.

From where I stood watching the unusual procession, I heard chunk-chunk-chunk. It was a man with a wooden leg, not an artificial limb, just a wooden stump that went chunk-chunk-chunk as he silently plodded along, and not far behind him came a man on crutches.

I stood at a corner of a street where the Company offices were. As marchers reached the corner, I noticed eyes glance up at the building and then straight ahead as they marched on. There was no word of complaint uttered, but tragedy was written upon each face, and I said to myself as I stood there, "And some wonder why there is class hatred."

Services were held at the grave, and as the casket was being lowered, friends passed by and placed a red carnation on the top of the already bloom-covered casket.

Chapter Sixteen

MAINLY ABOUT HOUSES

Even in architecture, Butte is not like any other city in the world, for here and there one will find a touch of Serb, Greek, Italian and English; also some attractive Swiss and other designs. Two Irishmen, who made fortunes, built beautiful places, Southern Colonial in design, such as one would see on large estates, but not in cities.

Towards the center of the city from these two places, there are three houses, Spanish in architecture. They stand on a rise of ground called Hibernian Terrace, and on a corner further in is a house patterned after a wing of a French chateau, and close by is a combination of arts, but no harmonious whole; the color scheme is good.

And then as we follow on to the east side of the city, we see a touch of Chinese. Near Timber Butte one will see a curl of blue smoke coming from an Indian tepee, and at the foot of Big Butte stands an attractive Dutch Colonial.

The most artistic residence in the city is one on the brow of a knoll called "Lovers' Roost." It is patterned after a

…chalet and built entirely of manganese and silver ore, and at times when the atmosphere is clear and the sun rays bright, the color effect is beautiful.

The house, patterned after a wing of a French chateau, was built by a son of a multi-millionaire. The young man married and went to Europe for the honeymoon, and it was while on this trip they saw and admired the old chateau.

When the house was finished, there was no lawn surrounding it, for it was erected at a time when grass would not grow in the city, and house-plants could not live if a window was left open, for the leaves of plants would turn yellow and then wither and dry. So the young people had the yard flagged with cobble-stone.

Even the shamrock does not blossom in its natural color, no matter how well it is guarded. A relative in the Old Country sent a box of shamrock roots and some soil to a relative in Butte. The roots were planted and protected in every way. At last, sprouts appeared above the earth, and there was great rejoicing in the neighborhood, for they were soon to see the real shamrock blossom. Buds came, and then sorrow, for the blossom was yellow. Some laid it to the sulphur fumes, others to the influence of a Cornish colony close by.

In the young millionaire's home there was a beautiful library finished in bird's-eye maple, and in the other part of the house the woodwork was mahogany and old ivory. The house has changed owners several times. The second owners made many changes. One day I was asked to go over and see the improvements. When I went in I was staggered to see what had been done. White enamel paint had been put over the beautiful old ivory. "I never could get the paint to look clean," said the occupant, in speaking of the old ivory. And when she showed me the library, she said, "You know, mahogany is so 'swell.' " She had stained the bird's-eye maple.

When people became rich on short notice, it seemed to be the heart's desire to live in this house.

The drawing-room was a large octagonal apartment, and anything but easy to furnish. The first owners had some handsome pieces of Louis the Fourteenth and Sixteenth, and antique tapestries, and the room was very attractive. But those following did not know. One day I met one of the occupants of later years standing looking into the window of an Oriental rug store. I stopped to speak with her. "Are you buying rugs this morning?" I asked. "I should say not," she answered, in much spirit. "None of them things for me. I think this fellow be a fake, so I do, an' I heered he were a camel driver in his own country. He persuaded us to take some of 'em on approval, so he did, an' he come up an' put 'em down hisself. He didn't tack 'em down, an' they wouldn't lay straight. One day I wint into the parlor, so I did, an' me fate slipt an' I wint down an' almost unther the middle rug. The old man came runnin' up, so he did, to say phwat were the matter, an' whin I looked up, he were a-slidin' across the floor on one of thim Sherooks; an' we sent 'em all back. I wint down town, so I did, an' had a foine one made, an' had it made round to fit the room. I don't care much fer thim polished floors, fer ivery toime I mop up the dust I have to polish thim agin, so I do."

"Look at this one, now," she said, pointing to a pretty Beluchistan, "an' see if ye don't think he be a fake. It's two or three shades lighter at this end than it be at the other."

As we stood talking, a man who had just made a "clean up" and bought a pretty home, came along and said to me,

"You are just the man I want to see. Come into Samoleon's with me. My wife wants an Oriental rug, and I want you to help me select it."

The dealer first showed him a beautiful Royal-Bokhara. "These are all fine Orientals," he said, as he displayed a handsome Kirmanshah and Shiraz. He did not seem pleased with any that had been shown to him. The dealer brought out another, and while unfolding it said, "Now, this is the finest Turkish I have in the house." The customer said, as he waved his hand, "You needn't unfold it, she has her heart set on an Oriental."

A market called City Public Market has been established in the city, and is a mass of architecture in itself. When I went down the hill to this market the first glimpse of the place sort of staggered me, and I said to myself, "How incongruous," and my mind at once traveled back to Italy and the Appian Way, a road leading into Rome, and an afternoon I was out for a drive and stopped at an old tomb that had been swept out and made a living place for a family, while another had been converted into a store where bits of things were sold.

In chapter "Wandering Around" I describe the section of the city where this market is located. The little one-room shacks huddled close together and close to the edge of the sidewalk are the small "cribs" where in early days unfortunates stood in the doorway and solicited. They have been made into booths where groceries, meats and other produce is sold.

BUTTE OF YESTERDAY

On the outer edge of the sidewalk, small stalls are built, half over a portion of the walk and part in the street. The front of the stalls faced the doors of the "cribs" and a roof built over the walk from the stalls to the "cribs," gave it a decidedly foreign appearance, and resembled market-places in poorer sections of foreign cities, such as Petticoat Alley in the Whitechapel district of London, where Saturday nights one can buy anything from a piano to a pig's snout, and Paddy's Market in Cork, where on Saturday marketers flock to buy provisions for the Sabbath day.

When I entered the passageway, the first booth I stopped at was occupied by a Finnish woman. I said to her, "Much like Helsingfors?"

At first she was surprised. "You know Helsingfors?" she smiled pleasantly. "Yes, it does; but not as large," she said, as I turned to take notice of a Russian Jew who came slowly along. He wore the long beard and Derby hat pulled low on the head, so characteristic of his race, and the Prince Albert coat and gold hoop earrings were not forgotten. True, the coat was old and bedraggled, and the hat faded and dusty, nevertheless it was the costume, and I said to the woman I had been talking with, "I must leave you, for here comes Moscow."

He was pleasant and smiled when I said to him: "My man, you should be pushing a cart filled with jewelry, pretty laces, some corset-covers and gay-colored ribbons."

"I see you have been in my country," he smiled, and passed on.

I also slowly walked along, stopping here and there, and in imagination again visiting the markets of Venice, Palermo, Algiers and other interesting places.

In the early sixties, a few prospectors, looking for gold, pitched their tents on the site that is now Butte. And a little later, and some farther up the side of the hill, a few log cabins were built and the camp staked out and named Butte City, for it was near a barren hill called Big Butte, and so the spectacular city of Butte was born to become the most noted camp in the world, and about fifty-two nationalities are represented today, and their influence adds to the picturesqueness of the camp.

Many there are who have memory and love for the Fatherland, and this is shown in the architecture of their homes.

I remember seeing the modest home of a Greek. In front of the little three-room cottage were two columns, one at either side of the door. They were made out of the trunks of pine trees—trunks that had been barked and placed in position to represent Corinthian columns. It showed the inborn love for columnar architecture. I noticed at the top of one column some crude carving made to represent acanthus leaves.

Chapter Seventeen

THE PLAGUE

The tragedy of a great disaster is no novelty in Butte. Again and again anxious throngs have passed around the openings to the mine shafts, or watched the slow curling smoke wreaths, that told of death to the workers imprisoned thousands of feet below. But in after years the plague of 1918 will be recorded as Butte's greatest tragedy. Early in the year there were rumors of the appearance of a new and virulent plague that threatened the world. It first appeared in Europe, then came to us. Climatic conditions did not effect it. It scourged every land and clime—the polar regions and the tropics.

It had been very violent among the Esquimaux of northern Alaska, while Papeete, the principal city of Tahiti—an island just south of the Equator, lost twenty per cent of its population, and here in America its first toll was well over half a million. The "black death" of the fourteenth century alone in history compares with the Plague of 1918-19, although of a vastly different nature. During the scourge of "black death" Italy lost one-half of her population. At that time the masses of Switzerland were without education and, as is usually the case with such people, superstition was uppermost and the Jews were accused of poisoning the wells. This intensified religious fanaticism and persecutions followed. The peacock feather, the symbol of the Jews, was not allowed worn and all the peacocks in the land were killed. That is why, by many, the peacock feather is considered unlucky.

In many localities, after losing its virulence, the present disease returns in a more virulent form. There seems to be three germs, each with characteristics peculiarly its own. The three distinct types of disease are both contagious and infectious.

Owing to the cosmopolitan population, Butte was the most advantageous place to study the disease; so interesting to watch and work with different temperaments. Foreigners, especially those of the Latin countries, are more nervous and excitable. Grab them mentally, if possible, and by so doing make the delirium less violent or death easier. While they are being prepared for bed, try and get the extent of their education, their station in life, their trend of thought, and by so doing, it is easier to help them through the crisis. Knowing the patient, one can more easily give the mental suggestion. The "Flu" is more than one-third mental. Many without temperature or a symptom of the disease died of fright. Many developed general malaise and gradually sank away.

As a rule, the disease develops rapidly, reaching its crisis in about three days. Another form, the patient feels miserable for a few days, but does not know the cause. He would pooh-pooh the suggestion of plague until at last it reaches the heart and he dies suddenly; some drop in the street.

A large airy schoolhouse was turned over to the Red Cross for a hospital as the city hospitals were all filled. When the hospital was opened to receive patients, the school teachers and a few other volunteer women came together as one. They were there to cook, they were there to nurse. They were God's noble women—there to do anything in their power for the sufferers. They were in the kitchen and sick rooms, banded together in true womanhood, working night and day with a zeal surpassed by none.

In the office were two men: one, a true man reared under the blue skies, with the pure air of the west to breathe, a possessor of sincere friendship and love of humanity; the other of foreign birth, small and delicate in stature, with a finesse such as Oscar Wilde possessed when he made his initial tour of America, a time when he wore knickerbockers and a sunflower in the lapel of his coat; a time when he made the startling announcement, "A kitchen stove is the most horrible thing I can look at." It was necessary for the nurses to carry through the corridors commodities used in the sick rooms. The young man's artistic temperament revolted and he was soon taken to his bed.

The ambulance was kept busy night and day bringing in the sick. Doctors' cars stood in front of the main entrance at all times. There was a back door and a side door where the undertakers came. Patients who were able to stand alone when they left the ambulance at the front door seemed dazed; some were emaciated from hunger and long attempt to care for themselves.

One handsome young fellow said to me, as he came in: "Doctor, will you give me a sandwich? I am, oh! so hungry." He did not live long; there was not enough left to work on.

In one ward, two days after the hospital opened its doors to receive patients, in the west end of the large room, was

a row of five beds, each bed containing a delirious
patient—strong, robust men, and across the narrow aisle
were four cots with as many delirious patients. Out of the
nine we saved four. They were all desperately sick and
most of them violently delirious. This ward was a splendid
illustration of Butte's cosmopolitan population for, at one
time, I remember, there were several Austrians, a Mormon,
two Greeks, two Irishmen, a Cornishman, a Jew, two
Americans, a Finn, an Italian, a Polander, a Slav and a
Swede.

One night it was necessary to give an Italian a hypodermic
of morphine; he was becoming violently delirious. I was
holding him down trying to get his arm in a position where
he could not jerk and break the needle. As he felt the prick
of the needle he became very violent and bit me on the
arm. It was necessary to tie his hands and feet. Soon the
narcotic took effect and he fell asleep. For several days
after that, he would watch me closely as I passed around
the ward, and to some of those who came near him, he
would say, "I don't like the big fellow; he sticks needles in
me." He again became violent and very noisy, and it was
again necessary to give him a hypodermic. When he
quieted down, he said to me: "I feel better; I go to sleep;
when I wake up I be quiet." I had gained his confidence
and he got well. Whenever I would go near his cot he
would move his legs over to make room for me to sit
down.

A Polander lay desperately sick and delirious, but not
violent. In the forepart of the night several doctors said:
"You will send him to the undertaker's before morning."
About midnight the delirious man said to me: "Doctor, is
the war over?" I told him I thought so and that I was to be
President of Poland. "How splendid," he said, as he
brightened up. I asked him if he wanted to work for me.
"Yes," he said, "let's go back now," and he tried to leave

his bed. I told him he was sick, but we would go as soon as he got well, and he was to be my coachman. I asked him to try and help me make him well. I described the livery I was to have made for him and then he fell asleep. During the days that followed he would say to those who came near him, "The big doctor is to be President of Poland and I am going to work for him." A week or so later he left for Spokane a well man.

I said to a Greek who lay in a bed adjoining the Polander's: "Have you ever been through the Dardanelles?" He said, "Yes, many times." I put him in charge of a gun at the entrance of the Dardanelles and he watched it faithfully. Once in a while I would go to the side of his bed and say to him, "Son, I'm through with my work now and will watch the gun while you rest." He would fall asleep. He is a well man today.

One young fellow, nineteen years of age, was in such condition it was necessary to tie his feet to the bars at the foot of the bed, his hands at the side, and a strip of cloth under his chin and tied to the bars at the head of the bed. His doctor treated him with ice compresses. We tried every possible means to quiet him. At last I said to him: "Bill, I'm dreadfully busy and want you to look after this part of the ward and report to me when I return." He quieted down, and when I went to his bed some time later he said: "All those fellows have colds but one and he's a nut; he's got the 'flu.' " I told him I was all through with my work and would watch them while he got his rest, and he fell asleep. He is now back at work.

I believe most of the patients, although unable to give expression, are conscious up to the last. Gus, a Greek, bears me out in this. At the beginning of his sickness he did not sleep at all, was noisy, and sang a great deal in an undertone. Hypodermics had no effect upon him. I asked him to try counting sheep jumping over a fence. He tried it before becoming delirious. He was about four days dying, and just before the breath left his body, I could hear him counting almost inaudibly, one, two, three; one, two, three came from the lips that were parched with tartian malaria.

An Austrian's death brought tears to many eyes. He was a handsome fellow, and a fine patient. Wonderfully educated. When asked his nationality, he said in a joshing way: "I'm a Scandinavian." As he was passing into delirium I said to him: "John, what part of Scandinavia are you from?" He looked at me and said, "For God's sake don't call me a Swede. I'm an Austrian." And from that time on, even after coming from delirium, he often spoke his native tongue.

One night he asked me to let him hold the rosary in his hands. "First," he said, "let us sing 'Over There.' " He had a good voice and sang a few lines of the patriotic song. His strength was on the wane and he could go no further. His nerves were active almost to the state of hysteria. "Daddy," he said, "may I have a cigarette?" I drew a screen partly around his cot and let him have one. Only one or two attempts to smoke and he laid it down. I asked him why he called me "Daddy." His answer was: "Because we love those who are kind to us." He asked me if I knew the story of the song, "The Rosary." When I told him I did, he said: "Tell it to me. I know it, but I want to hear you tell it."

He quietly listened as I told how Rodgers, the composer of the words, was inspired by an episode in his life, and how he found expression in the string of pearls, and of the romance and tragic death of the composer of the music. When I had finished he looked around and then said, "Daddy, draw the screen a little closer and come here." He then told me of the romance in his life, and the love story he told in Spanish was like a beautiful bouquet. They were the last rational words he spoke. Soon there were signs of meningitis, and in a few hours the undertaker came.

A young man from the Postal Telegraph office was an interesting patient. He was restless and kept trying to get out of bed. The forepart of one night he said to me, "I want to send a private message." I told him to lie back on his pillows and let me tuck his feet in and then he could send it. His right hand came out of the covers, and for a moment his fingers worked an imaginary ticker. Then he said, "Please look after the office while I send this Armour & Company code message to Spokane." He then worked the imaginary ticker for about half an hour, and then said, "I'm tired—it's hard work, the phrasing is so difficult."

I told him I also was tired and asked him to go to sleep and let me go to bed, and in the morning we would straighten up things. He fell asleep. In about two hours I went in the ward again. He was sitting up in bed. One of the nurses said he had been asking for me. When I went to the side of his bed he said, "I have a thirteen hundred word message to send. Please help me."

He lay back on the pillow and closed his eyes while his fingers worked the imaginary ticker for a little over three-quarters of an hour, then he looked up at me and said, "It's finished. My work is done." Then closed his eyes and soon the undertaker came.

Many souls seemed too weak to release themselves from the body. One night, a hurry call came for me to go to a ward on the second floor. A man wished to make his will. A few days before I had sent his wife to the undertaker. When I went into that room the scene was worse than any picture of Dante's Inferno. The lights were dimmed by tissue paper. Patients were writhing and groaning in anguish, and a purple haze had settled over several who were passing away. A minister was making a spectacular prayer beside a patient's bed, while the nurses went quietly about their work. After I drew up his will and he signed it, he said, "I now feel better and will go to sleep." I laid him back on his pillow, and in a short time the undertaker came.

A bride and groom came from the northern part of the state. It was a sad honeymoon, for in a few hours after reaching Butte they both came to the hospital. He recovered, but took his bride home in a casket.

Little ones were sent to the undertakers, while parents struggled with death. Parents were taken to the undertakers leaving little ones in the nursery. Little families have gone together to the life beyond. One night a baby was born while on an adjoining cot a life flickered and passed away.

That same night a patient came in—a young man of about thirty years. The lights that hung from the ceiling were covered with different colored tissue paper. He seemed to be watching them. When I went to the side of his cot he said, "Doctor, is this an insane asylum?" I told him it was a hospital and the moans came from the sick. He quieted as his eyes turned back to the lights, covered with tissue, then turned to a nurse and said, "Will you let the canary birds sing for me?"

A most interesting patient was a young man seventeen years of age and engaged to be married to a sweet young girl. His face was handsome and strong, but younger than his years would indicate. His body was the making of a wonderful man physically. He loved flowers and the nurses were kind to keep him supplied. At times he was delirious, and then again he seemed to be just half-conscious. At one time when we thought he was wholly unconscious, I tried him out. I said to one of the nurses, who stood close by, "I think he is a Finlander." His eyes opened quickly as he turned to me and said, "No, I am Scotch Irish."

The evening before he died, I gave him a fresh carnation. All that night he held it in his hand. Once in a while he would seem to be looking for something—the carnation had dropped from his hand and he was searching for it.

His sweetheart came and stayed all that night, as did several other loved ones. When she first came in and stood by the side of his bed, his eyes seemed puzzled. He looked at me, then back at her. Recognition came. The hand with the carnation went out to her as he said, "Oh, Nell, it's you."

About midnight one of the nurses brought him a pink rose. He lay with the carnation in one hand and the rose in the other. At day-break I thought he was getting better and his friends went home. About nine o'clock I gave him a fresh carnation. He kissed the back of my hand and said, "Doctor, don't leave me—it will soon be over." His chin quivered as tears came to his eyes. The undertaker soon came.

A young man, whose limbs were rapidly failing, motioned to me to come to where he lay. "Nurse," he said in a low whisper, "you are strong, will you take me to the roof and toss me up in the pure air so I can breathe?" He soon smothered to death.

Chapter Eighteen

GOING DRY

The old Bohemian days have passed.
When the stakes of the game ran high,
And friendships counted a damn sight more
Than they do since the camp went dry.

From the *Sage of Butte*.

If Bethel had always been dry there never would have been
written the story of Jacob "seeing things." To really
appreciate that story, one should see the Stone of Scone,
which tradition identifies as the one upon which Jacob
rested his head. The stone is now beneath the seat of the
ancient coronation chair in Westminster Abbey. It is
supposed Jacob's son took the stone to Egypt, and King
Gathelus took it from there to Spain. It next appeared in
Ireland, being taken there by Simon Brech. It was placed
on the sacred hill of Tara and called "Lia-Fail," the "fatal"
stone or "stone of destiny." From there it found its way to
Scotland, where King Kenneth placed it in Scone. King
Edward I took it to England, where it now rests. It is a

stone, I should say, about ten by thirty inches and mightily uncomfortable looking for a pillow for a teetotaler.

Butte was supposed to have gone dry at midnight, December 30th, 1918. Many a time during previous years, the columns of the newspapers have contained declarations made by men holding high public office that the laws of the state against gambling, prostitution, road-houses and the like would henceforth be rigidly enforced. And, after a brief interval, these evils would be as rampant in the community as ever.

The Attorney General of Montana, in speaking of Butte and conditions in general, said, "Butte is going to be cleaned up and kept cleaned up. While I realize that Butte is a different town with a different class of people to handle than any other town in the state, this is no excuse for the conditions that exist there. Just the method to be employed, I am not yet ready to disclose, but plans are being matured and the work will be done, whether I get the help of the county and city officials or not."

Shortly after midnight a small-sized riot occurred at one resort and beer bottles and chairs were used with great energy. No one seemed to know who started the fight, but when the officers arrived everybody in the place seemed to have a hand in it.

Several were arrested on a disturbance charge, and the police then ordered every one out of the place. A detail of police was stationed at the front door after the disturbance to prevent any one entering.

Three wagons were kept busy most of the night bringing in drunks and men charged with disturbance. The emergency hospital was also a busy place, and the city physician and nurses treated many broken heads and bruised faces.

On the whole, it was a quiet night, considering the fact that it was the last night the saloons were supposed to be open in Butte. At the cabarets the question was not, "Will they sell drinks after midnight?" but, "Will there be any liquor left by midnight?"

About half a dozen of the most frequented bars announced during the afternoon that nothing stronger than beer was obtainable—everything stronger had been disposed of. In the places where "hard licker" was still to be had, patrons were lined in front of the bar in a double rank and the trade in bottled goods was as rushing as the bar patronage.

The first real convulsion in the death struggle of John Barleycorn was the day the armistice was signed. The evening of that day, when I was on my way to the Red Cross Hospital, I heard the sound of music. I turned and looked down Broadway and coming towards me was a band with a crowd in front and a crowd behind it, and leading the procession was a little fellow. I had never seen him intoxicated but twice before—one time when the president of a corporation was giving a barbecue at Columbia Gardens and drinks were free—and at another time at the old Silver Bow Club, when all who wished were at liberty to hover around the punch-bowl. Late that night a soldier said to me, "I have just been to a cabaret. I wonder if the husbands and wives will ever get straightened out and back to their right homes."

That night saw the first convulsion of the old friend and enemy. These spasms followed at intervals until the night of the thirtieth, when the patient gasped and struggled and passed into a state of coma and at midnight, while surrounded by devoted friends, flickered, passed away.

Soon after midnight, I went to the Club to attend the wake. A dance was being given that night to celebrate the advent of prohibition and wake the corpse of Barleycorn, and, as is usually the case, the unexpected happened. All eyes had been turned on the Silver Bow anticipating a rousing time, but it turned out to be one of the quietest affairs ever given at the Club. There were only a few drunks carried out and one or two broken bones. There were many people present, but all seemed uncertain of themselves and the whole affair lacked the brilliancy of former years. Newcomers hardly knew what to do, and for that reason, held back. Indecision permeated the air. A peculiar mental condition seemed to possess each one. Some argued, "It's because it is not New Year's eve." Others, "It is because the date was changed."

The following day I went there again, and on the bar stood a row of bottles labeled, "Grape Juice," "Bevo," and so on, and just behind those new faces was the old familiar motto. The lines differ somewhat from the original that hangs in "Ye Olde Cheshire Cheese" of London, a part of the old town that is fast disappearing off the face of the earth. It is where Dr. Johnson reigned supreme; a resort where Sir Oliver Goldsmith, Charles Dickens, and many others prominent in literature spent much time; where Nell Gwynne and Charles II often lunched together.

> *"If on thy theme I rightly think.*
> *There are five reasons why men drink:*
> *Good wine, a friend, because I'm dry.*
> *At least, I shall be bye-and-bye.*
> *Or any other reason why."*

While I was there, a man came in, looked around and said as he passed out, "How strange it seems. It is like a land without a flag—without an army." As be turned and left the cheerless room, I thought of Omar Khayyam's lines.

> "Then said another with a long-drawn sigh.
> My clay with long oblivion is gone dry;
> But fill me with the old familiar juice, Methinks
> I might recover bye-and-bye."

And so Butte, after a wet lifetime, signed up with the Prohibitionists and became a dry town with many a full-stocked cellar, and the "wash-boiler still" working fast.

There will be no more classy "joy rides" to the festive road-house; there will be no more gay parties around the roulette table or the faro bank. Members of the four hundred and the underworld will be segregated. There will be no more large tips to drivers for patiently sitting around all night waiting to drive merrymakers uptown. The largest tip ever given in Butte was given to "Fat Jack" by a multi-millionaire.

In early days Jack borrowed an amount of money from this man, who was a friend. The friend took the borrower's note for the sum. The paper was laid away and in time forgotten. In later years the loaner became one of Butte's wealthiest citizens.

One day recently he was looking over some old papers and came across the note he had long since forgotten. He put it in his pocket. He was to leave for California in a few days, and when the time for departure came, he called Jack by 'phone and said, "I want you to drive me to the Oregon Short Line." It was not an unusual call and Jack promptly responded. When they reached the station the old-time friend said, "How much do I owe you?" Jack quietly answered, "Two dollars." The friend said, "All right," and then took from his pocket the bit of paper and handed it to Jack with the words, "I'll give you this as a tip." With accrued interest, the amount ran into the thousands.

Homer Davenport, the famous cartoonist, who became acquainted with "Fat Jack" while visiting in the west, once rescued some Butte people, who were visiting in New York, from an embarrassing predicament when their identity as Butte residents was questioned. Hastily drawing a sketch of "Fat Jack," he submitted it to them with the assertion, "If you can tell me who this is, I'll know that you are from Butte."

"It's 'Fat Jack,' " they answered in chorus. He had drawn a splendid sketch of the tall, thin driver, not forgetting the rusty silk hat and ever-present cigar.

Jack looks out of place driving a taxi, and says to those who ask questions, "The old town has lost caste."

Chapter Nineteen

AT THE PRESENT TIME

At the present time young trees grow in the cemeteries. Monuments and attractive head-stones supplant some of the wooden crosses. Pansies grow where tansy weed used to hold full sway. A new Country Club graces the "Flat," where pretty bungalows are springing up like weeds grown after a spring shower, or should we say like dainty cactus blossoms on a desert.

Legislators have long since quit leaving their transoms open. "What's the use?" they say. Some leading citizens still have each other watched by plain clothes men, for suspicion permeates the air.

Invitations with R.S.V.P. are still issued to hangings, the last one taking place the early morning of January 14th, 1918. At the hour of the execution it was still dark. Three men were executed and long before that hour, men, women and children jostled each other to gain admittance to a place where they might see a human being put to death, and it was necessary to call out the militia to quiet the rioting.

Mr. *Judge JJ Lynch*

*Your presence is requested at Butte, Montana, on the
morning of Monday, January Fourteenth, in the Year of Our
Lord Nineteen Hundred and Eighteen, to witness the execution of*

JOHN O'NEILL
FRANK FISHER
SHERMAN POWELL

JOHN K. O'ROURKE
Sheriff of Silver Bow County, Montana.

R. S. V. P.

INVITATION TO HANGING

Now trees grow in some parts of the city, and there are
some pretty lawns and flowers. A new court-house stands
on the site of the old "Palace of Sorrows." Coming in
touch with nature, children will develop differently—green
leaves and flowers to look at and green swards to play on
instead of tailing dumps will take them from the metallic
and in their minds will come beauty instead of corruption.
With beauty and a clean wholesome mind, honor will
come and that gives nerve to drive away fear and soon
Butte will be a city where people do not speak in an
undertone or first look around to see if there is danger of
being overheard.

Fascination and tragedy seem to be written everywhere.
Fear is in the expression of many faces—a fear of some
one in power to injure or with money to corrupt. With it
all there is a something that draws one back to the place—
a fascination we cannot understand. Changes in the place
have been tragic.

The white man came from towards the morning light and the Indians followed the setting sun, and are now seldom seen except when brought into the city as witnesses in bootlegging cases. In a few short years their story will be told in the pages of a novel and pictured in the movies. No more wild doings of the picturesque cowboys or blare of the hurdy-gurdy, for Prohibition killed the inspiration.

The road-agent seems to stay, but is not as picturesque a character as in frontier times. There are some mighty good friendships left, but as a rule the word has been commercialized, and there is not the old standard of manhood in the place. The "bull-fence" is built around Company properties, and above this fence barb-wire is strung from pole to pole, and through the wire volts of electricity can be passed.

In early days the souvenir gatherers were in evidence as they are today. An enthusiastic collector located the grave of "Clubfoot George," one of the five bandits who were lynched in Virginia City in the early sixties. He disinterred the body, removed the deformed foot, had it preserved, and placed in a curio case. A gruesome souvenir of those scarlet days. "Fat Jack," bent with the weight of years, has folded his tent and gone to the Old Soldiers' Home in California.

As the stranger rides to his hotel he says to himself, "How many men seem to be out of work." It is not that; they merely are off shift and have few places to go, for there are no city parks or pleasant streets where they may walk, so they stand around on the sidewalks of the business center.

One morning, recently, I returned to the city after a short absence. The side of the mountain was wrapped in a blanket of unsullied snow that had fallen during the night. As the day grew brighter, columns of slate-colored smoke rose from the mine stacks and spread, forming a mauve-colored canopy over the city, and from this overhanging atmosphere, quietly—like a gentle snow—came flakes of soot.

That forenoon I went into a restaurant for my coffee. A truly frontier place where we sit on stools at a counter, and just beyond, several cooks stand at a large range. Instead of men waiters calling out for the cook to hear "Adam and Eve on a raft," when the patron ordered poached eggs on toast, or "Jew's funeral with hearse on the side," meaning roast pork with gravy on the side, attractive young women in black and white uniforms took the orders.

"What'll it be?" one asked, as I took my seat.

Receiving the order, she quietly turned and gave it to one of the men at the range.

While I sat there, a man came in and said in a sort of off-hand manner: "The bank on the corner has just been held up."

The statement seemed to cause no excitement amongst those at the counter. He then told me how a few weeks previous a lone bandit had held up a bank on the "Flat." He said it was in broad daylight and the bandit made the officers of the bank lie down on their stomachs and crawl into the vault, where he locked them in, and then took what money there was on the counters.

As he passed out another friend came in and said, with a smile playing over his face: "I've just been up to the Federal Court, where they've got a bunch up for illicit prescribing of 'dope.' "

I asked him what kind.

"Mostly morphine," he answered; "a pound or so at a time," he smiled.

During the afternoon, I met an officer who showed me a poor attempt at an early-day vigilante notice that had just been sent to an inoffensive citizen. It was a "Turn of the Tables," for the criminal was trying to frighten the other fellow. It was the work of a novice and showed a poor mind. The 3-7-77 was there, but in crude manner.

After leaving him, I slowly walked up the hill towards my club, and as I was nearing the building I saw a large automobile truck turn into a passageway between the Club and Court House and then stop. Officers had just raided a moonshiner's establishment. It was a private still in a residence. On the truck were two barrels filled with water and sugar fermentation, several boxes containing cans of Old Dixie molasses, cans filled with mash, a wash-boiler of fresh brew and a queer looking affair the officers told me was the still itself. It was about one-third filled with fresh ingredients and ready for work.

It was getting along towards evening, and the atmosphere was clear, and after stopping at the Club for a short time, I boarded an electric car that passed through Dublin Gulch and then over trestles on its way to the summit, winding around in view of the ruins of the old Lexington silver mine, in its day one of the greatest silver producers in the country, but today worked for zinc, and from the car window, as it climbed the mountain, I could see the semi-ruins of the old Alice and Moulton mines, both in early days great silver producers. And then we passed closer to the Lexington. In the very early days of the camp, the ore from this mine was sacked and shipped to Swansea, Wales, for treatment.

When the car reached the end of the line, twilight was coming on and I stayed on top to witness that pretty sight. As the sun settled behind the western range its bright rays rested on the snow-capped Highlands and the summit blazed like a jeweled crown, the whole scene making a picture of marvelous beauty.

In a few moments the scene changed to one so different, so weird and fascinating, but just as beautiful. The lights of the city and valley began to shine forth, some a bright flash, while others just a soft glimmer. The Great Divide took on a deeper hue and seemed to close in on the valley. Soon a passenger train came through a tunnel, and, like a jeweled snake, began to wend its way along the mountain side towards the city. The headlight of the engine, as it passed around curves, cast out rays of light like fire from a dragon's nostrils.

All at once the heavens were lighted by brilliant rays that came from what seemed to be a cascade of fire. It was the emptying from a high trestle of a carload of molten slag.

I watched the orange sun go down
And the world take on its crimson glow,
And through the haze I seemed to see
The Indian tents of long ago.

For today on the mesa the soldiers' tents
Supplant the Indian tepee.
And the white men thrive where the red man failed,
From the East to the Western sea.

No longer the dust off the buffalo herd
Is seen on the mighty range,
And of the antelope few are left
To witness the mightier change.

The engines puff where the ox-teams trod.
And the tall steel girders run
Beside the tracks where the buffalo bones
Bleach in the blistering sun.

For progress rules with a cold, hard hand.
And the old romance is dead
When stolid farmers plow the land
That once was the rangers' bed.

Her brow is stained by the metal crown
She has wrung from the land today—
But with wistful eyes some of us dream
Of the West that has passed away.

Made in United States
Troutdale, OR
11/02/2023

14237033R00083